God is Gay

The Straight Christian's Guide to the Gay Issue

C.S.Clement

Scripture quotations identified as **ASV** are from the American Standard Version by Public Domain.

Scripture quotations identified as **DBY** are from the Darby Translation by Public Domain, 1884.

Scripture quotations identified as **DRA** are from the Douay-Rheims 1899 American Edition by Public Domain.

Scripture quotations identified as **ESV** are from The Holy Bible, English Stand Version® (ESV®), copyright© 2001 by Crossway, a publishing ministry of Good News Publishers. Used by permission. All rights reserved.

Scripture quotations identified as **GW** are from GOD'S WORD.® GOD'S WORD is a copyrighted work of God's Word to the Nations, Quotations are used by permission. Copyright 1995 by God's Word to the Nations. All rights reserved.

Scripture quotations identified as **KJ21** are from The Holy Bible, 21st Century King James Version (KJ21®) Copyright © 1994 by Deuel Enterprises, Inc. Gary, SD 57237. Used by permission. All rights reserved.

Scripture quotations identified as **KJV** are from the King James Version, by Public Domain.

Scripture quotations identified as **MSG** are from The Message, Copyright © 1993, 2002, 2018 by Eugene H. Peterson. Used by permission of NavPress. All rights reserved. Represented by Tyndale House Publishers, Inc.

Scripture quotations identified as **NASB** are from the New American Standard Bible®, Copyright © 1960, 1962, 1963, 1968, 1971, 1972, 1973, 1975, 1977, 1995 by The Lockman Foundation. Used by permission. www.Lockman.org

Scripture quotations identified as **NIRV** (NIrV®) are taken from the HOLY BIBLE, NEW INTERNATIONAL READER›S VERSION ®. NIrV®. Copyright © 1995, 1996, 1998, 2014 by Biblica, Inc.®. Used by permission. All rights reserved worldwide. The "NIrV" and "New International Reader's Version" are trademarks registered in the United States Patent and Trademark Office by Biblica, Inc.®. Use of either trademark requires the permission of Biblica Inc.®.

Scripture quotations identified as **NIV** are taken from the Holy Bible, New Interna-

Front Cover Photograph by John Stewart, NYC, johnstuartstudio@gmail.com

Back Cover Photograph by Lea Lee, Paris and NYC, lealeeart@mail.com

Dedication and Thanks

I owe enormous thanks to my Bible teachers JM, KC, BW, JO, CD, and JP.

They have taught me the Word, how to read the Bible,

how to hear from God, and I am so grateful.

Thank you to my editors, David Andrews, Martin Lowenstein,

and Robert Bonardi.

Thank you to my friends who agreed to read this as it was evolving.

And I dedicate this book to TC who

I hope will be proud of the effort.

Table of Contents

Who I am and why I wrote this book...9

Start Here...15

God Made Gay - Proof 1...19

Hypocrisy - Proof 2...28

All - Proof 3..49

Love - Proof 4...84

Judging Others - Proof 5...105

Sexual Sin - Proof 6..124

The Law - Proof 7..147

Bonus - Gay Marriage...192

Next Step..205

Appendix...210

Who I am and
why I wrote this book

It may be a surprise to most people that the Bible says nothing against gay people. People cannot discriminate against homosexuals on the basis of their Christian beliefs.

I ask people: "What is the basis of your Christian beliefs?"

If they say "the Bible", I would suggest that they go to the original Hebrew and Greek texts, where there is no such admonition against homosexuals.

If they say "the teachings of Pastor So-and-So", then they have their own religion, and it's called *The Church of the Teachings of Pastor So-and-So.*

I haven't seen any mainstream preacher or teacher of the Word apply any kind of scholarly rigor to the Gay Issue in Christianity, a scriptural contradiction that sincere Bible-loving and Jesus-loving people blindly tip-toe around.

We have freedom of religion, but it's a pity that there are so many religions that think they are Christian, but are really a hodge-podge of Jesus and Pastor So-and-So.

Mainstream Christian doctrine has become toxic, feeding the masses the Word of God mixed with a touch of poison, calling homophobia the Word of God.

While doing research into certain scriptures that seem in a modern reading of the Word to clearly be against homosexuality, I discovered that the original Greek and Hebrew texts in these scriptures **are not** about homosexuality. And I discovered that other scriptures, supposedly not about homosexuals, **were** about gay people.

What was the hint that this might be so? The key was that all the scriptural teachings on basic Christian principals cannot be true and a teaching against homosexuality also be true. The Gospel cannot contradict itself. Something is wrong when large Christian denominations violate basic Christian mandates to teach that homosexuals cannot be Christians.

Shouldn't the Church get its biblical scholars to look into this problem and resolve it? Well, they haven't, so I did. I found out exactly where they are wrong. This is the first book that takes all the research conducted by various scholars and puts the information all in one place.

At least 22 U.S. Christian Denominations refuse to accept homosexuals. At the time of this writing there are 22 Christian denominations or more in the U.S. that refuse to ordain practicing homosexuals and most of these denominations also do not allow homosexuals as church members. https://en.wikipedia. org/wiki/List_of_Christian_denominational_positions_on_homosexuality *Retrieved 18 May 2020.*

I expect this list to significantly change as the truth of what the Bible actually says about our gay brothers and sisters is revealed as historical and Godly truth by all Christians. I am confident that these denominations would not wish to prove to the watching world that theirs is not actually a Christian denomination and adjust their doctrine to more accurately reflect the Word of God.

There are now 27 Bible translations that wrongly include the word *homosexual*. More and more publishers are producing translations of the Holy Bible that use the word *homosexual* and they are all wrong.

1954 AMPC Amplified Bible Classic Edition
1 Corinthians 6:9

1960 NASB New American Standard Bible
1 Corinthians 6:9, 1 Timothy 1:10

1965 RSVCE Revised Standard Version Catholic Edition
1 Corinthians 6:9

1969 WEB World English Bible
1 Corinthians 6:9, 1 Timothy 1:10

1971 TLB Living Bible
Leviticus 18:22, Leviticus 20:13, Deuteronomy 23:17-18,
1 Kings 14:24, 1 Corinthians 6:9, 1 Timothy 1:10

1973 NIV New International Version
1 Timothy 1:10

1979 NIVUK New International Version-UK
1 Timothy 1:10

1982 NKJV New King James Version
1 Corinthians 6:9

1992 GNT Good News Translation
1 Corinthians 6:9

1995 CEV Contemporary English Version
1 Corinthians 6:9, 1 Timothy 1:10

1995 GW GOD'S WORD Translation

1 Corinthians 6:9, 1 Timothy 1:10, Jude 1:7

1995 ISV International Standard Version

Judges 19:15, 1 Corinthians 6:9, 1 Timothy 1:10, Jude 1:7

1996 NET New English Translation

1 Corinthians 6:9, 1 Timothy 1:10

1996 NIRV New International Reader's Version

1 Timothy 1:10

1996 NLT New Living Translation

Leviticus 18:22, Leviticus 20:13, 1 Corinthians 6:9, 1 Timothy 1:10

1999 HCSB Holman Christian Standard Bible

1 Corinthians 6:9, 1 Timothy 1:10

2000 JUB Jubilee Bible 2000

1 Corinthians 6:9, 1 Timothy 1:10

2001 ESV English Standard Version

1 Corinthians 6:9, 1 Timothy 1:10

2006 ERV Easy-to-Read Version

1 Timothy 1:10

2011 DLNT Disciples' Literal New Testament

1 Corinthians 6:9, 1 Timothy 1:10

2011 EXB Expanded Bible

1 Corinthians 6:9-10, 1 Timothy 1:10

2011 MOUNCE Mounce Reverse-Interlinear New Testament

1 Corinthians 6:9, 1 Timothy 1:10

2011 NOG Names of God Bible
1 Corinthians 6:9, 1 Timothy 1:10, Jude 1:7

2012 LEB Lexham English Bible
1 Corinthians 6:9, 1 Timothy 1:10

2012 VOICE The Voice
1 Timothy 1:10

2014 MEV Modern English Version
1 Corinthians 6:9

2015 AMP Amplified Bible
1 Corinthians 6:9, 1 Timothy 1:10

These Bible publishers cannot even agree among themselves where in the Bible God meant to say *homosexual*. In these Bible translations, there are as few as a single *homosexual* reference to as many as six *homosexual* references.

And in no place where the original scriptures actually do refer to homosexuals does any published translation properly translate that text as *homosexual*.

That is why I wrote this book. I am not a pastor. I have never attended seminary, nor have I any degrees in theology. Yet, I may have the perfect set of credentials to write a book addressed to straight Christians to talk about the Gay Issue in Christianity.

I am the right age. I was born in 1951. I remember Christianity before it became a code word for *homophobia*.

I am the right sexual orientation. I am heterosexual. No one can say, based on my sexual orientation, that this book has a gay bias

I am statistically the most wrong person to write this book. According to a recent Pew Report, it seems I am one of the least likely people to support gay issues. Politically, I tend to be conservative. I am a white Evangelical Christian. I am from the South. Religious and political affiliations, plus my geographic marker, supposedly make me a unicorn in the pro-gay universe. But I doubt very much I am alone.

> Matthew 11:25 (NKJV)
>
> ... Jesus answered and said, "I thank You, Father, Lord of heaven and earth, that **You have hidden these things from *the* wise and prudent and have revealed them to babes.".**

Aren't there other books out there written along the same line? I have not seen this information from all these various sources organized into one book where all questions can be answered. After you read this book, write me and let me know if you agree or disagree with that statement. Just reach out to me on https://www.facebook.com/godisgay.thebook/

Free Gift – As a thank you for investing your time to read *God is Gay*, I want to give you a shareable version you can give to your friends or church group. Just click http://www.godisgay.com/free/ to download now.

Start Here

Does your Bible have the word homosexual in it?

If your Bible has the word *homosexual* in it, it's not authentic. It contains a lie designed to separate us from God.

The Old Testament was written in Hebrew from 1500 to 400 years before Christ. In those times, the Hebrew language had a word for what we today would call gay men. But this word has never been translated into the word *homosexual* in contemporary Bible translations. Other words that did not mean *homosexual* in Ancient Hebrew were erroneously translated as such in many contemporary Bibles.

In the Old Testament Hebrew there were no Hebrew words for *lesbian* and lesbians are not referenced in the Old Testament. When the New Testament was written in Ancient Greek, there were many Greek words for what we would call lesbians but none of these words appear in the New Testament.

The original Hebrew Old Testament and original Greek New Testament have no language aimed against homosexuals. When Biblical scholars first translated the original Hebrew and Greek texts into English they were faithful to the original. From the day that God first inspired man to write down his holy

Word, and up until 1954, there was no published Bible that contained the word *homosexual.*

The New Testament was written principally in Greek from 10 to 100 years after Christ. In those times, the Greek culture had words for straight men who had sex with other straight men and words for what we today call gay men. However, some of these words referring to straight male sex practices were erroneously translated into the word *homosexual* in contemporary Bible translations.

Since 1954, and with increasing frequency, many translators of the scriptures have taken liberties that proclaim the Bible says what it does not say and never said. This is the opposite of true scholarship.

The **Amplified Bible**, first published in 1954, was the first popular Bible translation to contain the word *homosexual.* It appeared once, in 1 Corinthians 6:9. The 1954 translation is now called the **Amplified Bible Classic Edition.** There is now a new translation, **The Amplified Bible,** published in 2015. The word *homosexual* appears in two instances, 1 Corinthians 6:9 and 1 Timothy 1:10.

The most popular Bible translation in America is the **King James Version**. This is a good, solid translation from the original Hebrew and Greek. However, the **New King James Version** is a creation of the Bible publishing company, Thomas Nelson, and it contains one instance of the word *homosexual* that is not in the original. I point this out in the event that you are looking at your home Bible and think the **King James Version** and the **New King James Version** are the same. They are not.

Translators who have decided to use *homosexual* in Biblical text cannot agree among themselves. In the many erroneous Bible translations, there are as few as a single *homosexual* reference to as many as six. But as you will learn, they are all wrong.

Proving that God is Gay.

God is gay and I can prove it. I'm going to walk you through God's word, the Holy Bible, and demonstrate to you, over and over again, that God made gay,

God loves gay, and God's plan for all of his gay sons and daughters is a good life and a place in his Kingdom.

In Chapter One, the **first point** that I'm going to prove is that God made gay and that we were not made to criticize any of God's creations

> Isaiah 45:9-12 (NRSV)
>
> Woe to you who strive with your Maker, earthen vessels with the Potter! Does the clay say to the one who fashions it, "What are you making?" or "Your work has no handles"? Woe to anyone who says to a father, "What are you begetting?" or to a woman, "With what are you in labor?" **Thus says the Lord, the Holy One of Israel, and its Maker: will you question me about my children or command me concerning the work of my hands?** I made the earth, and created humankind upon it; it was my hands that stretched out the heavens, and I commanded all their host.

To criticize another person and to single them out, saying that they are made wrong and their very existence is against God's Word, is nothing new. This happened back in Biblical times, too. And that's why we have this admonishment that since God made us all, to criticize someone is to criticize God, who made every person.

God created nature and gay is natural. We see it in the animal population with every species, so how can we call our human brothers and sisters who are gay *unnatural*? Having sex with someone you are not attracted to is unnatural.

In Chapter Two, the **second point** I will prove is that anyone who points to the Bible as evidence that being gay is against God's will is a hypocrite. and a detestable thing before God. All those who claim that being homosexual is a sin and therefore outside the Christian way of life is a card-carrying Pharisee, not a follower of Jesus Christ.

In Chapter Three, the **third point** I will prove is that God's love is for all. Jesus did not turn to the thief on the cross, promising he would see him in Paradise, but then say "Unless, of course, you're gay." I will prove that homosexuals are in the Bible and that they are included in God's plans for us all.

In Chapter Four, the **fourth point** I will prove is that we are commanded to love one another and to not criticize each other. Anti-gay finger wagging from the pulpit is not love. The old Christian saw, "Love the sinner, hate the sin," is a sentiment that cannot apply if the alleged *sin* is something that is intrinsic to that person such as gender, eye-color, or height.

In Chapter Five, the **fifth point** is that God commands us through his holy Word to not judge our brothers and sisters. To judge others is to usurp God's sole authority and is, therefore, wrong.

In Chapter Six, the **sixth point** is to expressly peel back the meaning of the term *sexual immorality* and *sexual sin,* since those terms have been misinterpreted as representing homosexual behavior. In fact, *sexual immorality* means using or abusing another person for one's own selfish gratification. There is no language in the Bible that refers to gay sex.

In Chapter Seven, the **seventh point** I will prove, that God embraces gay, is an exploration of the law. The scriptures used today to allegedly prove that God is against gays are part of the laws handed down by Moses, but based on faulty translations usurp the original scriptural intent. I also explore why God gave mankind the law and what place the law holds for us now that Christ has fulfilled the law.

God Made Gay - Proof 1

**God made us all in his image —
gay, lesbian, straight, bisexual, and transgender.**

In the beginning, God made the world, and at some point afterward he made humankind. And since God made humankind, he made every kind of human. And we are all made in his image.

> Genesis 1:26 (KJV)
>
> And God said, **Let us make man in our image**, after our likeness: and let them have dominion over the fish of the sea, and over the fowl of the air, and over the cattle, and over all the earth, and over every creeping thing that creepeth upon the earth.

> Genesis 5:1 (KJV)
>
> This is the book of the generations of Adam. In the day that God created man, **in the likeness of God made he him**;

Therefore, it is accurate to say God is black since black men and women are made in his image. God made brown and white and every shade and race. Therefore it is accurate to say God is white. He is brown. He is female. He is male. Every shade and race of humankind is a reflection of God since these were made in his image. And as gay men and women were made in his image, God is gay.

> Revelation 4:11 (KJV)
>
> Thou art worthy, O Lord, to receive glory and honour and power: **for thou hast created all things**, and for thy pleasure they are and were created.

> John 1:3 (KJV)
>
> **All things were made by him**; and without him was not anything made that was made.

Historically the Bible has been misused to support many kinds of bigotry, and homophobia is but the last gasp of this unscriptural perversion of the Word of God.

The world we know today is a world of entrenched bigotry. In every corner of this world, since the beginning of time, there has existed some form of bigotry in every known civilization ever recorded. Historically, certain pastors have used the Bible to support bigotry including racism, sexism, and anti-Semitism.

For centuries Bible verses have been used to 'prove' that God considers the black race inferior.

Bible verses have been used to 'prove' that God forbids women to preach or speak in church or to behave independently of their husbands.

Bible verses have been used to 'prove' that Jews are not going to heaven.

Bible verses have been used to 'prove' that slavery is part of God's plan for certain peoples.

Bible verses have been used to 'prove' that God puts poverty and sickness on people to teach them lessons and for his own glory.

Now Bible verses are being used to 'prove' that God does not love his gay children and that homosexual men and women are outside of God's plan.

In order to fabricate such a lie that is so clearly contrary to what the Bible actually says, it's critical that those who proclaim this twisted thinking must first lay their own unscriptural groundwork. And that unscriptural lie is that sexual orientation is a conscious choice. There is no scripture on which to base this idea and yet I heard a preacher who said from the pulpit that a certain man had **decided** to take up the homosexual lifestyle and he, therefore, was going against God's law. Seems to me then that this preacher should say to his wife, "I want you to know I chose you because I wanted to follow God's law but I could just as easily have chosen your brother. So I hope you respect my choice to be heterosexual because I am only choosing you, a woman, as my marriage partner, because I wish to conform to scriptural teachings, not because I have any genuine sexual interest in you."

That sounds ridiculous because it is ridiculous. Approximately 99% of the people in the world have some sexual orientation. Perhaps 90% of the population is of heterosexual orientation but they could not at any time say that this was a choice. So of the perhaps 9% of the population who are of homosexual orientation, it must also be said that this was not a choice. Sexual orientation is never a choice.

Made that way.

Throughout the Bible — in the Old Testament and in the New Testament — God has impressed upon his people that he has made each of us from before the foundation of the world. God has said over and over again in his Word that he knew us before we were born, that he made us by his own design. We were blessed before we were born and our children are blessed before they are born.

Psalm 147:12-13 (NRSV)

Praise the Lord, O Jerusalem! Praise your God, O Zion! For he strengthens the bars of your gates; **he blesses your children within you**.

Jeremiah 1:5 (NASB)

Before I formed you in the womb I knew you, and **before you were born I consecrated you**;

Isaiah 44:2 (ESV)

Thus says the Lord who made you, who **formed you in the womb and will help you**.

Isaiah 49:1 (NRSV)

The Lord called me before I was born, while I was in my mother's womb he named me.

Isaiah 49:5 (NRSV)

And now the Lord says, **who formed me in the womb to be his servant**, to bring Jacob back to him, and that Israel might be gathered to him, for I'm honored in the sight of the Lord, and my God has become my strength.

Psalm 119:73 (NRSV)

Your hands have made and fashioned me; give me understanding that I may learn your Commandments.

God made some of us gay. But we are not to argue about it, not to God or anyone else.

Isaiah 29:16 (NRSV)

Shall the thing made say of its maker, "He did not make me", or the thing formed say of the one who formed it, "He has no understanding"?

Romans 9:20 (NRSV)

But who indeed are you, a human being, to argue with God? **Will what is molded say to the one who holds it, "Why have you made me like this?"**

Malachi 2:10 (NRSV)

Have we not all one father? Has not one God created us? Why then are we faithless to one another, profaning the covenant of our ancestors?

God made gay and God made straight. How can anyone then not embrace his gay brothers and sisters who are from God?

> **God is inclusive and there is no disqualification in his Word for any of us.**

In the Scripture, when Jesus is nailed to the cross and the thief on the cross next to him speaks to Jesus and asks for his blessing, Jesus says to him, "This day you will be with me in Paradise — unless, of course, you are gay." Just kidding. That's not what Jesus said.

Matthew 10:32 (NRSV)

Everyone therefore who acknowledges me before others, I also will knowledge before my Father in heaven; but whoever denies me before others, I also deny before my Father in heaven.

In this Scripture, Jesus does not say, "Everyone who would acknowledge me before others, I also will acknowledge before my father in heaven — unless, of course, they are gay."

Matthew 11:4-5 (NRSV)

Jesus answered them, "**Go and tell John what you hear and see: the blind receive their sight, the lame walk, the lepers are cleansed, the deaf hear, the dead are raised, and the poor have good news brought them.**"

Again, Jesus did not say, "The blind receive their sight, the lame walk, the lepers are cleansed, the deaf hear, the dead are raised — unless, of course, they are gay, in which case, not so much."

In all of Jesus' healing, he never healed anyone from homosexuality. Of all of the afflictions that have been identified in the Bible as conditions that required correction, none of these conditions resemble same-sex attraction.

> Acts 11:9 (NRSV)
>
> But a second time the voice answered from heaven, "**what God has made clean, you must not call profane.**"

God made everything so God made gay. That is the Bible. All that God made — the work of his hands — he loves, and is precious to him, and we are forbidden to profane any of his good works.

All of God's promises are inclusive and we are all — all of us — implied in all references to blessings he provides us. In Isaiah 61 it does NOT say —

> The spirit of the Lord God is upon me, because the Lord has anointed me; he has sent me to bring good news to the oppressed **unless they are gay,**
>
> to bind up the brokenhearted **unless they are gay,**
>
> to proclaim liberty to the captives **unless they are gay,**
>
> and release to the prisoners **unless they are gay.**
>
> Because their shame was double, and dishonor was proclaimed as their lot, therefore they shall possess a double portion **unless they are gay,**
>
> everlasting joy shall be theirs **unless they are gay.**
>
> For I the Lord love justice, I hate robbery and wrong doing; I will faithfully give them their recompense **unless they are gay,**

and I will make an everlasting covenant with them **unless they are gay**.

The above is NOT the Word of God and yet there are many who act as though it is the Word of God. To have a classification of persons to whom these scriptures do not apply would mean we must add to the Bible to make it so. And to add to the Word of God is forbidden:

Deuteronomy 4:2 (RSV)

You shall not add to the word which I command you, nor take from it; that you may keep the commandments of the Lord your God which I command you.

Deuteronomy 12:32 (KJV)

What thing soever I command you, observe to do it: **thou shalt not add thereto, nor diminish from it.**

Psalms 119:160 (KJV)

Thy word is true from the beginning: and every one of thy righteous judgments endureth forever.

Proverbs 30:5-6 (KJV)

Every word of God is pure: he is a shield unto them that put their trust in him. **Add thou not unto his words, lest he reprove thee, and thou be found a liar.**

Taking the Word of God and the Truth of our Lord Jesus Christ and perverting it to fit the politics or trends or traditions or cultural bigotry of the day has always been a problem. It was a problem in Paul's day, too:

Galatians 1:6-12 (NIV)

I am astonished that you are so quickly deserting the one who called you by the grace of Christ **and are turning to a**

different gospel— which is really no gospel at all. Evidently some people are throwing you into confusion and are trying to pervert the gospel of Christ. But even if we or an angel from heaven should preach a gospel other than the one we preached to you, let him be eternally condemned! As we have already said, so now I say again: **If anybody is preaching to you a gospel other than what you accepted, let him be eternally condemned!** Am I now trying to win the approval of men, or of God? Or am I trying to please men? If I were still trying to please men, I would not be a servant of Christ. I want you to know, brothers, **that the gospel I preached is not something that man made up.** I did not receive it from any man, nor was I taught it; rather, I received it by revelation from Jesus Christ.

The Bible is God-inspired and as such is able to hold together the intent of the Father even through the imperfect handling of man and even across millennia.

> **When we serve our gay brothers and sisters, we are serving Jesus who is one of them.**

Jesus walked this Earth to teach us and he taught us *through his actions* that he is Lord, triumphant, and God's own. But by his words he taught us that he would forever walk this Earth as the least of us.

Matthew 25:35-46 (KJV)

For I was an hungered, and ye gave me meat: I was thirsty, and ye gave me drink: I was a stranger, and ye took me in: Naked, and ye clothed me: I was sick, and ye visited me: I was in prison, and ye came unto me. Then shall the righteous answer him, saying, Lord, when saw we thee hungered, and fed thee? Or thirsty, and gave thee drink? When saw we thee a stranger, and took thee in? Or naked, and clothed thee? When saw we thee sick, or in prison, and came unto thee? And the King shall answer and say unto them, **Verily I say unto you, Inasmuch as ye have done it unto one of the least**

of these my brethren, ye have done it unto me. Then shall he say also unto them on the left hand, Depart from me, ye cursed, into everlasting fire, prepared for the devil and his angels: For I was hungered, and ye gave me no meat: I was thirsty, and ye gave me no drink: I was a stranger, and ye took me not in: naked, and ye clothed me not: sick, and in prison, and ye visited me not. Then shall they also answer him, saying, Lord, when saw we thee hungered, or athirst, or a stranger, or naked, or sick, or in prison, and did not minister unto thee? Then shall he answer them, saying, **Verily I say unto you, Inasmuch as ye did it not to one of the least of these, ye did it not to me.** And these shall go away into everlasting punishment: but the righteous into life eternal.

So here Jesus is saying to us that he is the lonely prisoner, he is the hungry woman. Jesus is every abused, forgotten person that society shuns. Jesus is the bullied gay teenager. Jesus is the beaten cross-dresser, the lesbian single mother. Jesus is everyone society casts off, gay or straight. And you are not following him if you mistreat them.

Hypocrisy - Proof 2

Hypocrisy is the most powerful tool for destroying people's faith in God and in the Bible.

Gandhi said, "I like your Christ. I do not like your Christians. They are so unlike your Christ."

Christianity has been hijacked by people who do not represent Jesus accurately. We have all experienced it. The Christian 'brand' has been co-opted by many factions and individuals, including well-meaning relatives and ignorant others, until the words *Christian* and *Church* have become worse than meaningless. In the mainstream culture, the word *Christian* is shorthand for *sanctimonious* and *hypocritical*.

What is so bad about hypocrisy? Isn't that just the blanket crime all teens accuse their parents of? Isn't that just a petty slander leveled at everyone in a position of authority? No, hypocrisy is killing our churches and losing souls that would otherwise see Christ. But they can't see Christ because they see hypocrisy in the guise of Christianity and turn away in disgust. *Hypocrisy* may seem to be small potatoes but it is deadly.

In any conversation about religion, the past crimes and the hypocrisy of the Church are easy targets, derailing any conversation from God to the short-comings of the Church. If, as followers of Christ, we represent to the world just another opinion of what's right and what's wrong, then we cannot claim to have anything better to offer than would a political party or a humanistic philosophy.

Hypocrisy misrepresents Jesus and misrepresents God.

What Jesus had to say that is so important is that God made us all, God loves us all, God is with us all, and God accepts us all. For the Church to practice anything less is hypocrisy—claiming to be one thing while being something else — claiming to be a follower of Christ while being something else.

The most glaring hypocrisy in the Church today, both Catholic and Protestant, is its leadership's almost unified stand against homosexuality. God made homosexual people.

John 1:3 (KJV)

All things were made by him; and without him was not any thing made that was made.

God made all of us in this world because he loves all of us.

John 3:16 (KJV)

For **God so loved the world**, that he gave his only begotten Son, that whosoever believeth in him should not perish, but have everlasting life.

All of this is proclaimed clearly in the Scriptures. So to misrepresent Christianity so outrageously to the world is to misrepresent Jesus and to misrepresent God.

Jesus warned us to beware of hypocrites, especially the religious authorities of the Church:

Luke 12:1 (NRSV)

Meanwhile, the crowd gathered by the thousands, so that they trampled on one another, he began to speak first of his disciples, "**Beware of the yeast of the Pharisees, that is, their hypocrisy.**"

The Pharisees in the time of Jesus were the fundamentalists in the Jewish religion of the day. Jesus often used the Pharisees as an example of how not to hear from God, how not to follow God's Word, how not to behave.

Luke 11:42 (NRSV)

"**But woe to you Pharisees!** For you tithe mint and rue and herbs of all kinds, **and neglect justice and the love of God**; it is these you ought to have practiced, without neglecting the others."

This quote from Jesus shows the Pharisees strictly following the religious rules but not being loving or just. They have not understood the meaning of the law of tithes and offerings which today represents God's Word on giving (Luke 6:38).

Luke 6:38 (KJV)

Give, and it shall be given unto you; good measure, pressed down, and shaken together, and running over, shall men give into your bosom. For with the same measure that ye mete withal it shall be measured to you again.

God says if you are exacting and legalistic with your money, God and people will be exacting and legalistic with you. Love and be generous to others and God and others will be loving and generous to you. The Message translation of this verse is more clear:

Luke 6:38 The Message (MSG)

"Don't pick on people, jump on their failures, criticize their faults—unless, of course, you want the same treatment. Don't condemn those who are down; that hardness can boomerang.

Be easy on people; you'll find life a lot easier. **Give away your life; you'll find life given back, but not merely given back — given back with bonus and blessing**. Giving, not getting, is the way. Generosity begets generosity."

Hypocrisy was one of the first issues of the Church at its very founding by the original followers of Christ. Jesus was a Jew and his first converts were Jews. But as the Jesus Movement grew and acquired Gentile believers, there were cultural issues to be sorted out. Many of the Jewish followers of Jesus were still following all the traditional Mosaic laws and rules and believed that these Gentiles were somehow a lower caste than themselves and should be treated as such. Paul instructed the early Church that this was hypocrisy.

> Galatians 2:11-16 (NRSV)
>
> But when Cephas came to Antioch, I opposed him to his face, because he stood self-condemned; for until certain people came from James, he used to eat with the Gentiles. But after they came, he drew back and kept himself separate for fear of the circumcision faction. **And the other Jews joined him in this hypocrisy, so that even Barnabas was led astray by their hypocrisy.** When I saw that they were not acting consistently with the truth of the gospel, I said to Cephas before them all, "If you, though a Jew, lived like a Gentile and not like a Jew, how can you compel the Gentiles to live like Jews?" We ourselves are Jews by birth and not Gentile sinners; yet we know that a person is justified not by the works of the law but through faith in Jesus Christ. And we have come to believe in Jesus Christ, so that we might be justified by faith in Christ, and not by doing the works of the law, because no one will be justified by the works the law.

The Gentiles of the early Church were the outcasts. In those days it was culturally understood that Gentiles were socially inferior to the Jews and it was OK to treat them as lower-class citizens. In this letter from Paul to the Galatians he relates the situation where the early Christians were falling back on their pre-Christian prejudices and traditions, not because they believe them to be right in their heart, but because they did not want other Jews to criticize them and think they are not good Jews. They didn't want to get kicked out of the 'Jewish Club.' The Scriptures and Jewish traditions of those times demanded that Jews set themselves apart from non-Jews and never take meals with Gentiles.

The Jews considered themselves superior to Gentiles in every way and not mixing socially with Gentiles was more than an ingrained practice, it was the outward sign of a long-held belief that Gentiles were godless and inferior. When David called out to Goliath, saying, "Who is this uncircumcised Philistine that he should defy the armies of the living God?" (1 Samuel 17:26 – ASV) he was cussing at Goliath. David spat out the term "uncircumcised" like a curse word at the giant. He was raining insults on him, and to point out that Goliath was not a Jew was, in David's mind, the supreme insult.

In Galatians, the early Jewish followers of Christ, understood through the teachings of Jesus that all people who love and follow Christ are the same—children of God and brothers and sisters to each other. But certain Jews of the day were scandalized by this behavior of their fellow Jews—eating with and mingling with Gentiles—so that certain Christian Jews felt pressured to return to their traditions and to separate themselves from their Gentile Christian brethren so as not to attract criticism from their fellow Jews.

This is an exact parallel to the gay issue in the Church today. Certain Christian ministers know that the Bible is true—that all who believe on Christ are one with Christ and each other. However, these ministers may find themselves giving in to pressure to continue to act toward gay Christians as if the Bible was not true and all that mattered was what people think. They are afraid to get kicked out of the 'Christian Club.' These are the hypocrites — the ones who know better and yet still act as if Jesus had not died on the cross for us all and went to Hell for us all and rose again for us all and is now seated in Heavenly places with us all and with the Father.

Hypocrisy is the criticism of others when you yourself are imperfect and may even have a terrible history and serious issues:

> Luke 6:41-42 (NRSV)
>
> Why do you see the speck in your neighbor's eye, but do not notice the log in your own eye? Or how can you say to your neighbor, "Friend, let me take out the speck in your eye," when you yourself do not see the log in your own eye? **You hypocrite, first take the log out of your own eye**, and then you will see clearly to take the speck out of your neighbor's eye.

We have no business criticizing each other. Each of us has an enormous project to work on every day of the world and it is called Being-A-Follower-Of-Christ. To do otherwise is to be a hypocrite. To be a hypocrite is to be like the world. To be like the world is to be like any political group, opinion maker, or philosopher.

Jesus was an enormous celebrity of his day and he was criticized constantly for being true to his teachings. In Matthew 11:19 Jesus says that he was called a glutton, a drunkard, and criticized for hanging around with the wrong crowd. But, although he was often vilified, he was no hypocrite.

By his example, Jesus is showing that it is wisdom to be with all people and a friend to all people and to care about all people. If Jesus walked the Earth in the flesh today he would be seen with movie stars, politicians, drug addicts, mobsters, and have fans in every level of society, gay and straight. This clearly would be a problem for many of today's Church leaders.

> Matthew 23:25 (NIV)
>
> **"Woe to you, teachers of the law and Pharisees, you hypocrites!** You clean the outside of the cup and dish, but inside they are full of greed and self-indulgence."

If you know what you are doing is right in the sight of God, just do it and do not even feel tempted to explain yourself to anyone.

Roman 14:22 (KJV)

Hast thou faith? Have it to thyself before God. **Happy is he that condemeth not himself in that thing which he alloweth.**

Paul advises the Church that if you know in your heart that what you are doing is right in the sight of God, then don't be troubled about it no matter what other Christians say. Have faith in what the Word of God says and you cannot waste time arguing with other so-called Christians.

Hypocrites hurt themselves because they are not in God's will.

If you disagree with someone's teaching, keep it to yourself. It is clear that God is the only one who can reveal the truth to them.

Matthew 23:1-12 (NRSV)

Then Jesus said to the crowds and to his disciples**, "The scribes and the Pharisees sit on Moses' seat; therefore, do whatever they teach you and follow it; but do not do as they do, for they do not practice what they teach.** They tie up heavy burdens, hard to bear, and lay them on the shoulders of others; but they themselves are unwilling to lift a finger to move them. They do all their deeds to be seen by others; for they make their phylacteries broad and their fringes long. They love to have the place of honor at banquets and the best seats in the synagogues, and to be greeted with respect in the marketplaces, and to have people call them rabbi. But you are not to be called rabbi, for you have one teacher, and you are all students. And call no one your father on earth, for you have one Father—the one in heaven. Nor are you to be called instructors, for you have one instructor, the Messiah. **The greatest among you will be your servant. All who exalt themselves will be humbled, and all who humble themselves will be exalted.**

Pastors can tell you what is 'God's best' and point to laws in the Bible and sound authoritative. And because they are Bible teachers, we are to respect them. But these people can never be models for how to live your life. Only Jesus can be our model of how to live.

When Jesus was alive on the earth, the Jews still sacrificed animals at the Temple. The Jewish religious traditions, rituals, and rules gave instructions on the proper way to execute even the smallest detail of daily life. Jesus is saying here to respect authority, but to understand there is a higher law than this. This higher law is a spiritual law and not about manmade rules, because not even the most highly placed authority in the Jewish synagogue of the day could follow all these rules themselves.

This means that, in the days of Jesus, everyone knew that the religious synagogue leaders were hypocrites. The Jewish religious leaders, the Pharisees, placed their focus on rituals and religious legalism. Jesus came to save us from a hypocritical Church, not to make a **new** hypocritical Church.

> Galatians 6:1-5 (ESV)
>
> Brothers, if anyone is caught in any transgression, you who are spiritual should restore him in a spirit of gentleness. Keep watch on yourself, lest you too be tempted. **Bear one another's burdens, and so fulfill the law of Christ. For if anyone thinks he is something, when he is nothing**, he deceives himself. But let each one test his own work, and then his reason to boast will be in himself alone and not in his neighbor. For each will have to bear his own load.

The Word of God is clear—we are to stay out of hypocrisy. And we do that through keeping in touch with a spirit of gentleness. We are to treat everyone respectfully, even if they do have goofy ideas that have little connection to spiritual truths.

How do these Bible teachers misrepresent God?
They think God is represented by the lists of sins.

What is the confusion driving hypocrisy? These Christian hypocrites think God and the lists in the scriptures are the same thing. They believe God is the same as the lists of *thou shall not*'s.

They think God is the list. They think that God is a set of rules and that to be loved by God, to be right with God, to be righteous, you have to live by these lists of sins to avoid — you have to obey the rules.

This is the lie that the entire Bible was written to uncover. Before the Bible there were lists of laws. Laws and rules are not the exclusive domain of God. Even the bus has rules (don't spit, don't smoke, don't litter). Having rules in this world does not denote a higher way of life. In fact, having rules and lists of what to do and what not to do is secular and common. The entire world can be organized into what one can and cannot do in any particular place at any particular time or for any particular reason: How to do your taxes, How to behave in the movie theatre, How to lose weight, How to drive your car, How to bake a cake, How to organize a birthday party, How to brush your teeth. The Bible—and its documentation of the many rules of those times—has perfectly captured the culture and mind-set of the ancient world through the lists of rules-to-live-by. Looking at these lists of rules in the Bible we can very easily see what they considered important.

The lists don't cover homosexuality.

So what are all these lists? The first list most people are aware of is the Ten Commandments. The Ten Commandments are in Exodus 20:1 - 17 and Deuteronomy 5:6 - 21. And there is nothing in these verses that can be con-strued as describing a sin for being gay.

There are many lists of sins in the Bible. Some are short, such as the sins listed by the prophet Jeremiah. In Jeremiah 29:22 - 23, the prophet Jeremiah wrote to the religious leaders and said their exile in Babylon was a curse sent to them by God because of their adultery and lying about what God had said to them. But none of the sinners Jeremiah addressed were cursed because they were gay.

In Ezekiel 33:25 - 26, the prophet Ezekiel addressed the same religious exiles in Babylon and listed their sins as eating meat with blood still in it, acknowledging idols, killing, depending on their swords (instead of God), and adultery. There is no crime of being gay in this list of sins.

Just before he addressed this specific group, the prophet Ezekiel addressed all the people in Israel, a very large population, and laid out all the sins that God has told him lead to death and put them out of favor with God (Ezekiel 18:1 - 13). These sins were robbery, eating food given to idols, adultery, not taking care of the poor and needy, not repaying loans, worshiping idols, charging interest on loans, shedding blood or doing other violence to a brother, or making an unfair decision between others.

However, in this communication to all of Israel, none of these sins are being gay or having gay sex.

King Solomon is credited with writing most of Proverbs, a book of God-inspired instruction. In Proverbs 6:16-19, Solomon says there are seven abominations: a proud look, telling lies, shedding innocent blood, coming up with wicked thoughts and plans, rushing to evil (to see it, talk about it), saying you saw something or heard something that you didn't see or hear, and sowing discord among others. Solomon doesn't mention being gay or gay sex in his list of abominations.

In Matthew 19:16 - 19, Jesus says to keep the commandments but only mentions seven commandments. None of these commandments mention being straight.

In the Book of Deuteronomy, written by Moses, there are hundreds of sins including making an idol and setting it up in secret (Deuteronomy 27:15), and having sex with your half-sister (Deuteronomy 27:22).

But — surprise! — Rebecca, Jacob's wife, kept idols (Genesis 31:34) and the founder of our faith, Abraham, was a sinner. Abraham's wife Sarah, was his half-sister, his father's daughter by another mother (Genesis 20:12). God gives Abraham a pass on this since Abraham took Sarah as his wife before the Mosaic laws were written, Moses was even born, so, technically, there was no official rule against it at that time.

> Romans 5:13 (GW)
>
> Sin was in the world before there were any laws. But no record of sin can be kept when there are no laws.

That's how rules are, as laws can vary from state to state and change over time. So laws must be seen in their context before we can know if they are enforceable. The law, as handed down by Moses, is no longer enforceable (see Chapter 7). But I am getting ahead of myself.

So who is a Christian hypocrite today? It is anyone who sets themselves up as someone who doesn't sin.

What were the important sins in the times of the Bible?

One of the most-mentioned sins in the Bible is **adultery**. The following scripture is Jesus' definition of adultery.

> Matthew 5:27-32 (NRSV)
>
> You have heard that it was said, "You shall not commit adultery." But I say to you that **everyone who looks at a woman with lust has already committed adultery with her in his heart.** If your right eye causes you to sin, tear it out and thrown away; it is better for you to lose one of your members than for your whole body to be thrown into hell. And if your right hand causes you to sin, cut it off and throw it away; It is better for you to lose one of your members than for your whole body to go into hell. It was also said, "Whoever divorces his wife, let him give her a certificate of divorce."

But I say to you that anyone who divorces his wife, except on the ground of unchastity, causes her to commit adultery; and whoever marries a divorced woman commits adultery.

Therefore, according to Jesus, pretty much everyone has committed adultery. That's the point. Some mainstream, well-known, preachers today are sinners by scriptural definition. A famous woman preacher you probably know divorced her first husband (for good reason) and re-married. So, according to Jesus' definition, her second husband has committed adultery by marrying her (Matthew 5:32), since it seems that a divorced woman cannot re-marry. A famous preacher who founded what is now a super church was divorced and re-married before his success in his ministry. And a well-known televangelist has a daughter from a previous relationship, not with his famous wife. These are all my favorite preachers and I love and respect them.

I am not pointing fingers! I am making the point that what the Bible says is true! We all have sinned, according to the scriptures! Don't get touchy. I'm talking about me, too, of course. Even the most celebrated, conscientious, super-public religious leaders of our day have sinned and they will be the first ones to agree with me.

According to the scriptures above, even lusting in my heart for some movie star makes me an adulterer. Look at the description of adultery Jesus gave us in Matthew 5:27-32. It covers just about everyone at any vulnerable time in his or her life. A little baby is born. You look into the tiny face of that little pink or blue-hatted bundle and you can say with certitude, "Hey Little Guy (or Gal), you are born to be an adulterer." That sounds shocking, but it's true. And I only bring up that terrible image of the adulterer baby to make the point that the Bible spends hundreds of pages to make—that we are all sinners, every one of us (yes even your sainted granny and Mother Teresa) and that is why we cannot even *talk* about each other's shortcomings, ever. We all have that in common. We are all sinners, guaranteed. No one's perfect except Jesus. Get over it.

Is one sin worse than the others?

Some sins are no big deal, right? Wrong. According to scripture, if you break one teenie-weenie law somewhere, you have screwed up the whole thing.

> James 2: 10 (KJV)
>
> For whosoever shall keep the whole law, and yet offend in one point, he is guilty of all.

But some prophets have considered some laws worse than others. Jeremiah singles out the sin of adultery and lying as the most corrupting of sins:

> Jeremiah 9:2-6 (NRSV)
>
> O that I had in the desert a traveler's lodging place, that I might leave my people and go away from them! **For they are all adulterers, a band of traitors.** They bend their tongues like bows; they have grown strong in the land for falsehood, and not for truth; for they proceed from evil to evil, and they do not know me, says the Lord. Beware of your neighbors, and put no trust in any of your kin; for all your kin are supplanters, and every neighbor goes around like a slanderer. They all deceive their neighbors, **and no one speaks the truth**; they have taught their tongues to speak lies; they commit iniquity and are too weary to repent. Oppression upon oppression, deceit upon deceit! They refuse to know me, says the Lord.

Note that throughout the Bible, the most often noted sins are related to adultery and lying. But Abraham was an adulterer and a liar (him again), and even King David was a famous adulterer. Yet God said David was a man "after His own heart" and Abraham was God's "friend." It is obvious that being a sinner does not remove you from God's love or even his inner circle (if there is one). It is just the way things are. More clearly, it is the way we are. So all this compulsion to compare sins—how *my* sin is not *really* a sin (like mixing wool and linen, Leviticus 19:19, Deuteronomy 22:11) or how this sin cannot really be a sin at all (having sexual relations during the woman's menses, Leviticus 18:19, Leviticus 20:18, Ezekiel 22:10, Ezekiel 18:5 - 6) or how *your* sin is *so big* (like maybe murder) that I have the right to tell you whether you are going to Hell or not. But this is *not* what the Bible says. If you can't admit that you are a sinner, then you are a hypocrite. Admit it.

> ## Hypocrites like the sin lists because they think they are not on the list.

Hypocrites were in the Church in Jesus' day and hypocrites are in the Church now. Then and now, these hypocrites act as though they are not on the sin lists so they set themselves up as superior to others. But what folly that is, then and now, since these hypocrites are absolutely not able to keep all these rules.

Galatians 6:11-14 (NRSV)

See what large letters I make when I'm writing in my own hand! It is those who want to make a good showing in the flesh that try to compel you to be circumcised – only that they may not be persecuted for the cross of Christ. **Even the circumcised do not themselves obey the law (the Jewish church leaders)**, but they want you to be circumcised so that they may boast about your flesh. May I never boast except in the cross of our Lord Jesus Christ, through which the world has been crucified to me, and I to the world.

Everyone is on the list.

1 John 1:8-10 (KJV)

If we say that we have no sin, we deceive ourselves, and the truth is not in us. If we confess our sins, he is faithful and just to forgive us **our** sins and cleanse us from all unrighteousness. If we say that we have not sinned, we make him a liar, and his word is not in us.

That's the point—we are all on the list.

If you have done anything wrong that is on the list even *once* (Not kept the Sabbath? Lusted in your heart over anyone?) then you are a sinner. You have no right to point fingers at anyone ever in your whole life, because we are not to ever be the accuser. According to the Bible, that is someone else's job. Satan is called the "accuser of the brethren," not you.

> Revelation 12:10 (KJV)
>
> And I heard a loud voice saying in heaven, Now is come salvation, and strength, and the kingdom of our God, and the power of his Christ: for the **accuser of our brethren is cast down, which accused them before our God day and night.**

Jesus came to bring us life, not anything that is in the Devil's bag of tricks:

> John 10:10 (ESV)
>
> The thief comes only to steal and kill and destroy; **I have come that they may have life, and have it abundantly.**

The bar chart on page 44 shows that sin is God's way of humbling all of us.

So we have a very wide range of sins in the Bible from gathering sticks on the Sabbath (punishable by death) to murder (also punishable by death) to not obeying your mom (also punishable by death).

Since pretty much all Biblical sins are punishable by death, how do we know which sins were considered most important to the culture in Biblical times? Simple. By looking at the sins in the Bible and noting the number of times they are mentioned, it is simple to determine which sins were considered important by the people of the times in which the Bible was written.

As an example, today's current law books may only cover a specific crime with a single law, but a perusal of the current media will reveal what is considered important by the population. What is in the news? What is the hot topic in the TV-Movie-Of-The-Week? Murder, adultery, robbery, and greed are huge issues in today's media. But jaywalking?

The most often cited sin in the scriptures is lying (being a liar, having a lying tongue, telling falsehoods, bearing false witness, false lips). Lying is mentioned 119 times in the Bible as being wicked and sinful.

At the other end of the spectrum there are four scriptures that specifically warn against men and women having sexual relations during a woman's period and call it a sin warranting death. (The Bible says this act is an abomination and that God hates it—Leviticus 18:19, Leviticus 20:18, Ezekiel 22:10, Ezekiel 18:5-6). There are three scriptures that specifically warn against a man having sex with another man (Leviticus 18:22, Roman 1:27, Leviticus 20:13). And the sin of wearing a garment made of both wool and linen is mentioned twice (Leviticus 19:19, Deuteronomy 22:11).

And there are many sins that are mentioned only once (sowing mixed grain on the plot of land, tattoos, the law of disposing of human waste) etc.

By a simple count, the most cited sin in the Bible is lying. It beats out murder and adultery with twice as many mentions. But of all the sins in this bar chart, the only sin that any contemporary Church doctrines have singled out as a bar to Church inclusion, is sex between same-sex partners.

Which doesn't make sense.

Hypocrites.

Oh no!! So God is against gay sex?

NO and I will prove that later (see Chapter 3 and Chapter 6) but don't miss the point we are making here. The point of the law and sin is to prove to us all that we are all the same. We are all sinners. So we can stop comparing ourselves to

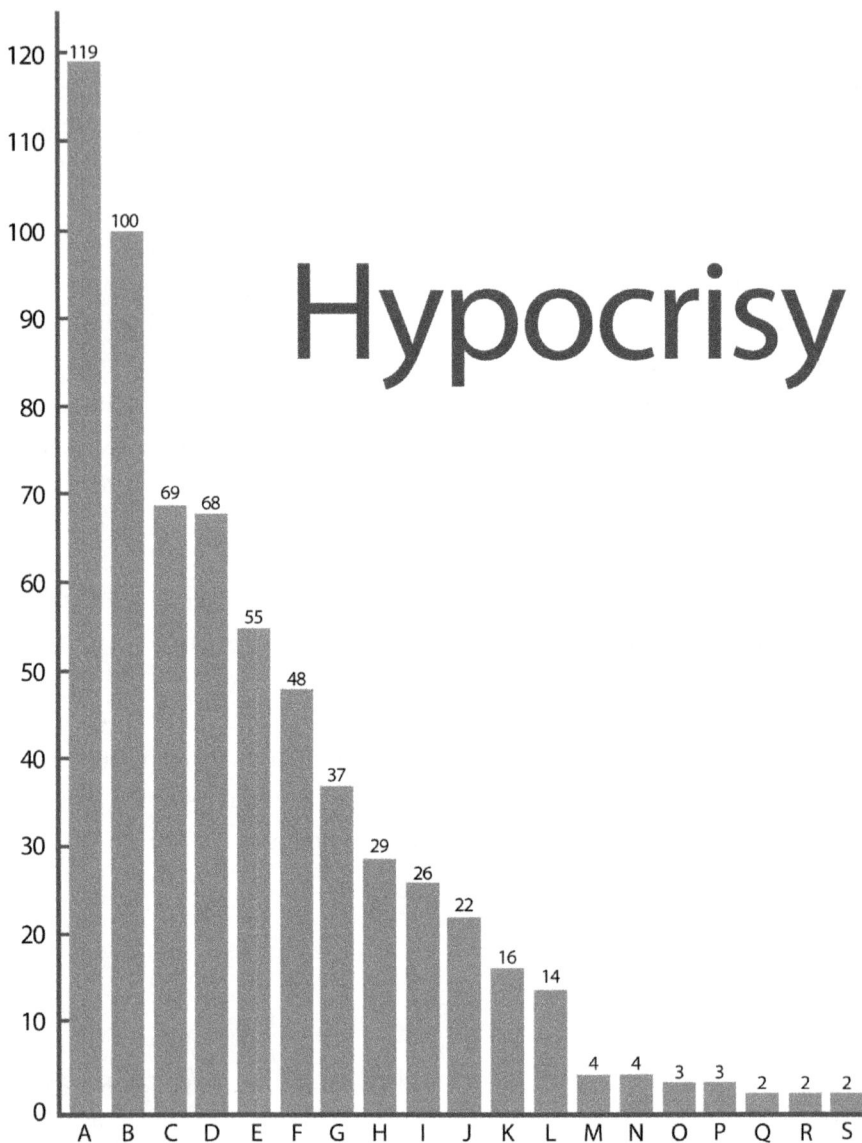

Hypocrisy

A   Lying (liar, lying tongue, falsehoods, false witness, false lips)—119 times

B   Being an idolater, idol worshipping, worshipping the Baals—100 times

C   Adultery, defiling neighbor's wife—69 times

D   Steal, cheat, or rob—68 times

E   Not keeping the Sabbath—55 times

F   Murder, shedding of innocent blood—48 times

G   Being a hypocrite—37 times

H   Gluttony or drunkenness—29 times

I   Covetousness—26 times

J   Seeing close family members naked—22 times

K   Misusing and profaning the Name of the Lord—16 times

L   Child sacrifice—14 times

M   Dishonoring your father and your mother—4 times

N   Having sex with your wife when she is in her period—4 times

O   Reaping your fields and not leaving the corners—3 times

P   Sex act between men—3 times

Q   Beating your slave to death or to serious injury—2 times

R   Wearing a garment woven of both wool and linen—2 times

S   Sowing discord—2 times

each other—stop thinking that any of us are better than anyone else—and get on with loving each other. Are you reading a magazine or washing dishes on Sunday (or whatever day is your Sabbath?). Busted. Ooops — break one and you might as well have broken them all. So you are a sinner — no better than anyone one else in this world.

The Sin Bar Chart above proves any church that preaches against homosexuality is hypocritical.

The Bible itself holds that all sin is the same—a stain upon the idea of perfection. So any pastor who leap-frogs over the hundreds of sins mentioned in the Bible to focus on one so-called sin for special treatment, any pastor who overlooks the importance the writers of the Bible gave other sins to select one obscure and rarely mentioned *alleged* sin, is showing the world that he or she is a hypocrite.

Is God really going to create gay people and then slap them around for acting on their natural God-given sexual orientation?

There is a legal term: _Arguendo_. It means *for argument's sake,* to pursue an argument in the alternative without admitting even the slightest possibility that those assumptions could be true. Homosexuality is not a sin and it will be demonstrated in this book that the Bible has never stated that homosexuality is a sin. But to make the case clear, I am proving that it is hypocritical for anyone in the Church to claim that homosexuality is a sin deserving of special treatment.

I am stating that, *arguendo*, homosexuality, for the purposes of making this point, is a sin. It is not. But if it were, it would still make no sense for the Church to single out that sin when what has been erroneously translated as *homosexuality* is barely touched upon in the scriptures especially when the entire congregation is bursting with sins that are pointedly singled out in the Bible.

Interpreting scripture through scripture.

So look at the bar chart. What feature jumps out at you? The 119 citations for lying is what jumps out at me.

Imagine for a minute that all the Christian churches decided that the sin of *lying* was a bar to being a Christian. The result would be empty churches. Adultery? Empty churches. Now see that category called *murder*? There are ministries tripping over each other to minister to residents on Death Row. What about the *gluttony / drunkenness* category? That area is almost ten times larger than the alleged *gay* category. What's wrong with this picture? What does it scream at us?

Manmade hypocrisy.

Every one of us looking at this chart sees themselves (now, or past and, certainly, future) committing sin, sin, sin. Maybe none of our sins will land us in jail or even raise an eyebrow at a PTA meeting. But that's not the point. What about that poor guy stoned to death for collecting sticks on the Sabbath? (Numbers 15: 32-36). Oops. That could be me, not keeping the Sabbath.

My point? We are all sinners. It is not a hard concept. We are all just too vain to accept it. That's the point the Bible is making. After you get it—that the Bible is pointing a finger at *you*—then you know you cannot point the finger at anyone else or you will certainly be a hypocrite.

There is not one area on this bar chart, not one class of sinner that a Christian church would reject except the so-called *gay* category. Why?

I submit that *gay* is the last area of bigotry in the Church that most of the Christian denominations can agree upon (and their Jewish and Muslim counterparts will agree with them, too!). It appeals to the basest part of our human nature—to build ourselves up by tearing someone else down. True, in some churches they are still struggling with the woman issue, the race issue, rap music, tattoos, and haircuts. But this is the last holdout that almost all the churches and religions can all pile on.

Hypocrites.

Timeless man in a backward world.

In the Old Testament, gay issues are not part of the Ten Commandments. In the New Testament, Jesus never healed anyone of homosexuality. He didn't agree with much of what was going on in the established religious institutions in his day, but Jesus instructed us to deal gently with each other and to not get upset with or disrespect the Church authorities.

So are we just to sit on our hands while established churches continue to preach anti-gay policies and claim they speak for God?

Be a follower of Christ, not a hypocrite.

The word *Church* means all of us together, the body of Jesus' followers, our community. Would it be a good thing if there were more people in the world who were following Jesus? Would this be a good thing? Yes, of course it would be. Even Gandhi would have joined the Church if the Church were actually a reflection of Jesus. But it is not. One cannot be like Jesus and be a hypocrite.

All - Proof 3

The Bible totally qualifies every human being on Earth as a child of God. All means all.

To re-cap, Jesus was hanging on the cross and the dying man who was on the cross next to him asked Jesus to remember him when he comes into his kingdom. And Jesus replied, "Truly I say, today you will be with me in paradise, unless, of course, you are gay."

Just kidding. Jesus would never say that.

In Luke 23:43 Jesus promises the dying thief a life with him in Paradise—no qualifiers. Jesus did not disqualify anyone with his offer of redemption and salvation.

The Bible says God made us **all** in his image, like God. The thief on the cross was made in God's image.

> Genesis 1:26 (KJV)
>
> Let us make man **in our image**.

This scripture is the basis for claims that God is black or God is brown or God is female. Race, gender, eye color, height, and sexual orientation are all aspects of human variety. God made all these varieties. All these varieties are facets of God's image. Humankind, in all our rich diversity, are all images of God.

John 1:3 (KJV)

All things were made by Him and without Him not any thing made that was made.

All means all. There is no disqualification. We are *all* God's creation.

A famous televangelist speaking about homosexuality was quoted as saying that "God wouldn't create anything that he says in his Word is an abomination." The televangelist was trying to say that homosexuality is a choice. Since I know for a fact there is only one God and he made everything that was made, then that preacher must actually be saying that homosexuals are NOT an abomination since God made them. Ha ha.

I don't think that's what he *meant* to say but, actually, that is what he *did* say (unless he is saying that there is no such thing as homosexuality).

Hebrews 2:6-8 (NRSV)

Someone has testified somewhere, 'What are human beings that you are mindful of them, or mortals, that you care for them? **You have made them** for a little while lower than the angels; you have crowned him with glory and honor, subjecting all things under their feet.

Other translations say, "For thou hast made him a little less than God (ASV.)"

And who are these men (and women and children)? They are all of us—black, gay, white, straight, brown, yellow, red—God did not rule out anyone.

> **God's promises are for all—promises to love us, promises to save us, promises that we are his children.**

Jesus was known for being totally inclusive as demonstrated in Mark 11:14 where the Pharisees asked him "Teacher, we know that you are sincere, and show deference to no one; for you do not regard people with partiality, but teach the way of God in accordance with truth (NRSV)."

Here Jesus is acknowledged as someone who treats everyone the same, who receives everyone the same way because, as he has said, "I only do what I see my Father do and I only say what I hear my Father say" (paraphrase of John 5:19, John 5:30, John 6:38, John 8:28, John 12:49 - 50, John 14:10).

Acts 2:21 (NRSV)

Everyone (includes gay) who calls on the name of the Lord shall be saved.

1 Timothy 2:3-6 (NRSV)

This is right and acceptable in the sight of God our Savior, who desires **everyone** (includes gay) to be saved and to come to the knowledge of the truth. For there is one God; there is also one mediator between God and humankind, Christ Jesus, himself human, who gave himself a ransom for **all**.

Psalm 70:4 (NRSV)

Let **all** (includes gay) who seek you rejoice and be glad in you. Let those who love your salvation say evermore, "God is great!"

Psalm 145:18-20 (NRSV)

The Lord is near to **all** who call on him (includes gay), to **all** who call on him in truth. He fulfills the desire of **all** who fear him (includes gay) he also hears their cry, and saves them (includes gay). The Lord watches over **all** who love him (includes gay)...

This verse says that God takes care of all who love him. He will also be near all who call out to Him. He will also fulfill the desires of all who fear (respect) him.

1 John 5:1 (NRSV)

Everyone who believes that Jesus is the Christ has been born of God (includes gay) and everyone who loves the parent loves the child.

1 John 5:12 (NRSV)

Whoever has the son has life (includes gay)...

All means all. "Whosoever" also means all. "Everybody" means all.

John 3:16 (KJV)

For God so loved the world that He gave His only begotten son, that **whosoever** believes in him should not perish but have everlasting life.

Romans 10:13-17 (KJV)

For **whosoever** shall call upon the name of the Lord shall be saved.

John 1:12 (NKJV)

But as **many** (means **all**) as received Him, to them He gave the right to become children of God, to those who believe in his name.

1 John 4:4 (NRSV)

Little children, you (**all**) are from God, and had conquered them; for the one who is in you is greater than the one who is in the world.

When the Bible says *man* it means *all.*

In the verse above, in First John, the Bible refers to all of us as little children. The Bible also refers to all of us as *man.* This means tall man, short man, tall woman, gay man, gay woman ..... all of us.

Psalm 37:23 (NASB)

The steps of a **man** are established by the Lord and he delights in his way.

This verse is often quoted as "the steps of a **good** man" because that is how it reads in the King James Version. Note that, in the King James Version, any word in italics means that that word was not in the original, and that it was added by the translators. So in this instance, the word *good* was added by the translators.

So if you think that you are not included in this verse because you are not *good*, then you are mistaken. Your steps and my steps are established by God, even though we are imperfect.

> Romans 8:31-32 (KJV)
>
> If God is for us, who is against us? He who did not withhold his own Son, but delivered him up for **all** of us, how shall he not with him also freely give us all things?

> Acts 16:30-31 (NRSV)
>
> "Sirs, what must I do to be saved?" They answered, "Believe on the Lord Jesus, and **you** will be saved, **you** and your household."

You means *all*. *You* is you and I and the cross-dresser and the transsexual.

> Galatians 3:28 (NRSV)
>
> There is no longer Jew or Greek, there is no longer slave or free, there is no longer male and female; for **all** of you are one in Christ Jesus.

Considering that some Christians have characterized the apostle Paul as a misogynist, it's important to note here he is saying that men and women, males and females, are all included in every aspect of our Christian walk. That is to say that gender has no part of any restriction on our life with Jesus nor can sexual orientation be a qualifier.

> Psalm 68:5 (NRSV)
>
> **Father of orphans and protector of widows** is God in his holy habitation.

Can a gay man be an orphan? Of course. Can a gay woman be a widow? Of course. Therefore, in every instance in the Bible when the Scriptures refer to someone and that person is meant to represent all of mankind—all of us—there is never a qualifier on that person. If it were otherwise, that scripture could not refer to all of mankind. If it were otherwise, the Bible could read something like this: "Do not speak harshly to an older man (unless he is gay) but speak to him as a father, to younger men (unless they are gay) as brothers, to older women (unless they are gay) as mothers, to younger women (unless they are gay) as sisters, with absolute purity" (*my silly version of 1 Timothy 5:1 - 2*).

Jesus is our highest authority in all matters.

When the Bible can seem to contradict itself, it is wise to look for the words of Jesus for clarity. The Old Testament is many books by many authors written over vast periods of time and it is holy. However, in a simple reading of the Old Testament, one may be led to believe that it is God who sends us sickness, and it is God who makes trouble in our lives. However, if it were God's will for us to be sick — if it was God who made us sick — then it would have been improper for Jesus to heal the sick. If it was God who brought trouble into our lives, it would have been improper for Jesus and the Old Testament prophets to bring financial miracles and other miracles in people's lives as it would be undoing the work of God who supposedly sent sickness, or sent financial ruin.

A clear example of this confusion is in the Old Testament that states that Moses permits divorce and there are even Biblical rules about how to affect a divorce (Deuteronomy 22:19, 22:20, 24:1 - 3). But the Bible says that God hates divorce (Malachi 2:16), and Jesus said that divorce is only in the scriptures because the Israelites insisted on it (Matthew 19:7 - 8).

Thus we know from the mouth of Jesus that people and their own human ideas have influenced Biblical writings and that, in the Bible, there are statements that are attributed to God that are not his.

When faced with these conflicts, we must use the entire Bible to interpret the Bible. We can trust Jesus as the final authority in all matters for he only does what he sees his Father do and he only says what he hears his Father say (John 5:19, John 5:30, John 6:38, John 8:28, John 12:49 - 50, John 14:10).

These are the words of Jesus:

> John 6:37 (NIRV)
>
> **Everyone** the Father gives me will come to me. I will never send away anyone who comes to me.

> John 17:20-21 (NRSV)
>
> I ask not only on behalf of these, but also on behalf of (**all**) those who will believe in me through their word, that they may **all** be one. As you, Father, are in me and I am in you, may they (**all**) also be in us, so that the world may believe that you have sent me.

God feels pretty strongly about his inclusion policies:

> Luke 17:2 (NRSV)
>
> It would be better for you if a millstone were hung around your neck and you are thrown into the sea than for you to cause one (**any**) of these little ones (**all new believers**) to stumble.

> Mark 9:42 (NRSV)
>
> If any of you put a stumbling block before (**any**) one of these little ones who believe in me, it would be better for you if the great millstone were hung around his neck and he were cast into the sea.

I could restate those last two Jesus quotes this way: "If you tell one gay teenager that God doesn't love him just the way he is, then you are in big trouble with God."

Why does God want the gay teen and the lesbian grandmother, the gay grandson? Because God needs them. God needs all of us. Every one of us was made just the way we were made because we need to be the way we are to fulfill our job as part of the body of Christ Jesus, which is his Church.

**The Old Testament agrees that
God made us all and saves us all.**

God has always included all of us, his children, in his plans and his protection and his support. Listen to him in the Old Testament:

Genesis 12:3 (KJV with my comments)

...and in thee shall **all** (gay and straight) families of the earth be blessed.

Psalm 146:8-10 (NRSV with my comments)

The Lord sets (**all**) the (gay and straight) prisoners free; the Lord opens the eyes of (**all**) the (gay and straight) blind. The Lord lifts up (**all**) those (gay and straight) who are bowed down; the Lord loves (**all**) the (gay and straight) righteous. The Lord watches over (**all**) the (gay and straight) strangers, he upholds (**all**) the (gay and straight) orphan(s) and (**all**) the (gay and straight) widow(s)...

Deuteronomy 10:17-19 (NRSV with my comments)

For the Lord your God is God of gods and Lord of lords, the great God, mighty and awesome who is not partial and takes no bribe, who executes justice for (**all**) the (gay and straight) orphan(s) and (**all**) the (gay and straight) widow(s), and who loves (**all**) the (gay and straight) strangers, providing them food and clothing. You shall also love the (gay and straight) stranger, for you were strangers (gay and straight) in the land of Egypt.

Jeremiah 31:34 (NRSV with my comments)

No longer shall they teach one another, or say to each other, "Know the Lord," for they shall **all** know me, from the least of them to the greatest, (from the gayest to the straightest) says the Lord; for I will forgive their iniquity, and remember their sin no more.

Isaiah 51:16 (NRSV with my comments)

I have put my words in your mouth, and hidden you (**all**) in the shadow of my hand, stretching out the heavens and laying the foundations of the earth, and saying to Zion, "You (gay and straight) are my people."

Isaiah 51:16 (NRSV with my comments)

The Lord redeems the life of his servants; **none** of those (gay or straight) who take refuge in him will be condemned.

> **Do not be taken in by people who say that homosexuals are not in Christ and are not part of the Church.**

It is God's will for all of us to not be lead astray by words from the pulpit or from anywhere else:

Colossians 2:2-4 (NRSV)

I want their hearts to be encouraged and united in love, so that they may have all the riches of assured understanding and have the knowledge of God's mystery, that is, Christ himself, in whom are hidden all the treasures of wisdom and knowledge. I am saying this so **that no one may deceive you with plausible arguments**.

Only listen to the words of Jesus, not anyone else who may mislead you with their pious-sounding but unscriptural Bible interpretations.

This pie chart graphs the simple truth of the Bible's single message—that God made us all and loves us all. There are no slices in this pie.

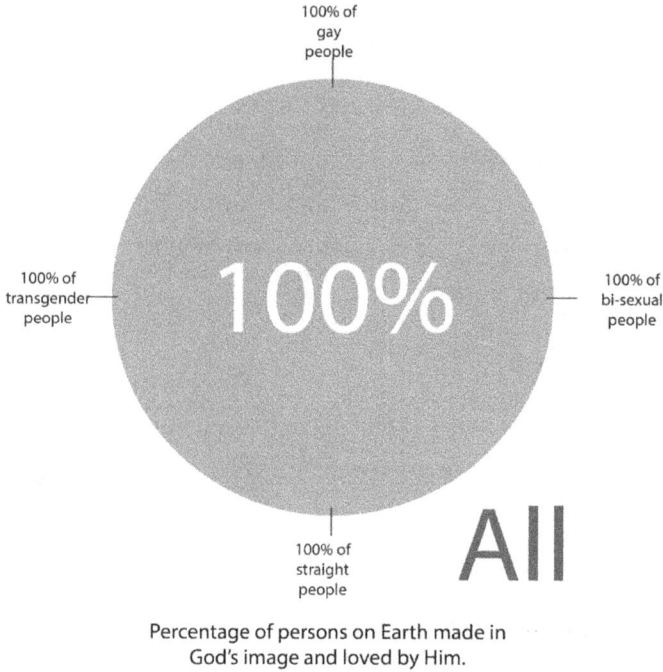

100% of
gay
people

100% of
transgender
people

100%

100% of
bi-sexual
people

All

100% of
straight
people

Percentage of persons on Earth made in
God's image and loved by Him.

**There have been gay men and woman throughout
history and in the Bible, too.**

The Bible cannot be read as a modern document. The ancient world in which it was written did not have the concepts of gay, straight, homosexual, and lesbian as we use them today. These are all relatively recent ideas.

The current concept of what is now called male homosexuality was not an accepted concept until 1897 through the efforts of Magnus Hirschfeld [*editor of 'Jahrbuch fur Sexuelle Zwischenstufen' (Annual for Sexual Intermediaries) 1899-1923*]. Shortly after the publishing of this work, in 1901 Hirschfeld published an article by Krafft-Ebing, the leading scholar of sexology of the day, wherein Krafft-Ebing admitted that homosexuality was always inborn and not pathological, as he had earlier claimed. The concept of a woman being a lesbian was not identified until the end of the 18th century [*London's Sapphists: From Three Sexes to Four Genders in the Making of Modern Culture, by Randolph Trumbach*].

However, male homosexuality (as we call it today) existed in ancient cultures but was called different names and was understood differently: New Guinea and its off-lying coastal societies had the *kwolu-aatmwol* (intersexed), India had the *hijras*, Polynesia had the *mahu*, Native North Americans had the *berdache* ["*Third Sex, Third Gender: Beyond Sexual Dimorphism in Culture and History*" Edited by Gilbert Herdt]. And, in the ancient lands of the Bible, that culture had the word *eunuch* to describe gay males.

The Byzantine Christians based the identity of eunuchs not entirely on physical facts—such as castration — but also on behavior and, more specifically, procreation. So by late antiquity the term *eunuch* had come to be applied to not just castrated men, but also men with comparable behavior, who had "chosen to withdraw from worldly activities and thus refused to procreate". ["*Wells, Collin. Review of The Perfect Servant: Eunuchs and the Social Construction of Gender in Byzantium, 2003 by Kathryn M. Ringrose*". Retrieved 2006-10-21]; ["*Review of Herdt, Gilbert (ed.) (1994) Third Sex, Third Gender: Beyond Sexual Dimorphism in Culture and History*". Retrieved 2006-10-21.]

It is basic to understand what is being said in the Bible if we are to know what God is saying to us today. To understand what God is saying about gay men and women today, we must know where gay men and women were in the Bible.

**The Three Genders in the Bible –
Male, Female, and Eunuch.**

In Biblical times, the thing that made one male was the ability to have sex with women and to have an interest in sex with women. What made a woman a woman was her ability to receive a man sexually.

A gay woman in this world was invisible as she would not seem different from a straight woman. As with any woman, the gay woman would be married off, would sexually receive her husband, and would bear children. To be a barren woman was certainly the worst thing a woman could be, worse than being a widow in this world where women had so few avenues to provide for themselves that did not include dependence upon a man. To be barren was considered a curse as there would be no son to provide for her in her old age. To be married and to have children was a basic survival strategy for all women.

And there was a third gender in these times, the eunuch. The eunuch was a physical male who did not exhibit the sexual interests of a typical male. Eunuchs had no interest in sex with women and, therefore, were quite useful for work with upper-class women (who could not be with any males except their master) or other work that was live-in as eunuchs were most often not married, and so required no housing for wives or children. These individuals were not burdened with the same expectations as males, had different social roles than males, and were identified openly as another gender, not male. In other words, eunuchs were considered a third sex. Legally and morally, males were permitted to have sex with any non-male, and non-males included females as well as eunuchs. More importantly, a man having sex with a eunuch would not expose himself to the legal responsibilities that accompanied having sex with a female. And a eunuch having sex with another eunuch would have no legal or moral impact.

Jesus calls gay men *Born Eunuchs*.

In Matthew 19:11 - 12 Jesus discussed marriage with his disciples, stating that marriage is the best state for most, but that eunuchs — those who are not interested in sex with women — should not marry. Then Jesus goes on to identify three types of eunuchs: born that way, made that way, and those who have made a personal choice to be celibate for spiritual reasons.

> Matthew 19:11-12 (written by Matthew in Palestine) (KJV)
>
> But he said unto them, All men cannot receive this saying, save they to whom it is given. **For there are some eunuchs,**

which were so born from their mother's womb: and there are some eunuchs, which were made eunuchs of men: and there be eunuchs, which have made themselves eunuchs for the kingdom of heaven's sake. He that is able to receive it, let him receive it.

Jesus is never random. The fact that Jesus has named these three groups in this order is noteworthy. The first group — Born Eunuchs — would be named first assumedly because this would be the largest group of individuals. These men were uninterested in sex with women and Jesus thought it important to advise that these individuals not marry. Therefore, since Jesus felt that he had to bring it up, we can know that certain born eunuchs *did* marry. Potiphar, a eunuch from the house of Pharaoh and Joseph's master in the Old Testament, was a married eunuch. However, when asked, Jesus advised against any eunuchs marrying. [*Clement of Alexandria stated that the beliefs of the disciples of Basilides, a Gnostic leader, about Matthew 19:12 was thus: "Some men, from their birth, have a nature to turn away from women; and those who are naturally constituted in this way do well not to marry. These, they say, are the eunuchs from birth." –from the original Greek, Clement of Alexandria, Stromata, III 1.1. Clement was born in 150 AD therefore his writings on this scripture are more contemporaneous to Jesus' statement and to Matthew's writing than any current commentary that state Jesus was referring to a rare type of birth defect.*]

These Born Eunuchs are who we would identify as gay men in contemporary times.

The next eunuch group Jesus advises not to marry is the group that he identified as Made Eunuchs. This was a much smaller group as the practice of castration was forbidden by Jewish Law and, in New Testament times, this practice was also criminalized by Roman Law. But there were still certain Made Eunuchs — castrated males — among the foreigners of those times who lived in the Biblical world. Jesus also advised this group not to marry.

The last group Jesus mentioned was the smallest group. It describes those individuals who, through dent of their spiritual focus, did not engage in sex with women by choice so they could commit themselves completely to the study and worship of God.

Many writers point out that this group included such spiritual individuals as Paul (who was unmarried) but it must also include Jesus himself. In Matthew 19:12, when Jesus is telling his disciples that people should marry except for those who are really devoting their lives to God, he would have had to include himself in this last group. After advising his followers that those fully committing their lives to God should not marry, Jesus would not then say "Oh, I don't mean *me*, of course. I mean someone like Bob in the next town. Man, he is *really* committing his life to God."

This is obviously silly. Jesus is the ideal of a human on this Earth who is fully devoting his life to God. Jesus has stated that he only says what he hears his Father say and he only does what he sees his Father do (John 5:19). So Jesus' every word and action has to have been premeditated which means constant meditation on the will of his heavenly Father. So Jesus was included in this last group. Jesus self-identified as a eunuch.

But this was not part of the contemporary nomenclature. Spiritual men of the Bible were not called *eunuchs*. In Bible times, gay men and castrated men were both identified as *eunuchs*. But men who remained unmarried because of their spiritual focus were not called *eunuchs*. Paul was called a *man* in the scriptures, not a *eunuch*, and he was unmarried because of his spiritual focus. Jesus was called a *man*. There is not anywhere in the Bible where a spiritual man is called a *eunuch*.

But it was Jesus' choice here, in Matthew 19:11 - 12, to call himself a eunuch to make a point that he has made elsewhere. In Matthew 25:35 - 40 Jesus identified as the thirsty, the hungry, and the naked poor, as the lonely prisoner or the sick. Jesus said here that he is all of us. And he also chose to say he is a eunuch, showing his solidarity with that group as he did with the other groups.

Though Jesus did say that gay men (Born Eunuchs) should not marry, he was only referring to marriage with women. Jesus' words cannot be contorted to exclude a committed marriage between same-sex couples as the Bible states that humans were not meant to be alone, that we were designed to have a partner to be happiest (Genesis 2:18; Ecclesiastes 4:8). At the time of his statement on marriage for Born Eunuchs, there was no concept of Earthly same-sex marriage.

How *Born Eunuchs* lived in the time of Jesus.

The Greek word for eunuch is *eunouchos*, but the Aramaic or Hebrew word for eunuch is *saris*. The word *saris* appears many times in the original Hebrew Old Testament.

Eunuchs are mentioned many times in the Bible using the Hebrew word *saris*. The Ancient Hebrews did not practice castration, but castrated eunuchs were common in other cultures featured in the Bible, such as Ancient Egypt, Babylonia, the Persian Empire and Ancient Rome.

But even before Jesus spoke in Matthew 19:11 - 12, the Jews of antiquity understood that there were different kinds of eunuchs. In the Tulmud, *eunuchs by nature*, Born Eunuchs, are *saris chmeh* and *eunuchs by castration*, Made Eunuchs, are called *saris adam* [*Yebamoth, VIII, folios 79b-84a*]. Notably, the King James Version translates the word *saris* sometimes as *chamberlain*, sometimes as *eunuch*, sometimes as *officer*, and sometimes as the name *Rabsaris* which really isn't anyone's name but is, rather, *chief eunuch*. But there are many other Hebrew words for the term *officers* so any translation of the word *eunuch* as *officer* is additional information about that person, a eunuch officer.

But in all these instances, the original word in Hebrew is *saris*—eunuch. This has led to further conjecture that many of these eunuchs (since they are all from the same word, *saris*) represent various types of eunuchs—gay men, and altered foreign slaves.

By studying the many scriptural instances of eunuchs (*saris*) in the Bible, we can see their social position, how eunuchs lived, and how they were considered.

Born Eunuchs **in the time of the Bible were fully integrated into all levels of society.**

Because castration was against Mosaic Law, most eunuchs in Biblical times who lived in the Biblical lands were Born Eunuchs, not castrated, **and some married**. In Biblical times, marriage was a desirable state and came with social and financial advantages. So, although these men were known to be eunuchs and, therefore, not male in the sexual sense, some eunuchs married. For example, Potiphar, Joseph's master, was married:

> Genesis 37:36 (written by Moses in the Wilderness) (YLT)
>
> And the Medanites have sold him unto Egypt, to Potiphar, **a eunuch of Pharaoh**, head of the executioners.

> Genesis 39:1 (written by Moses in the Wilderness) (YLT)
>
> And Joseph hath been brought down to Egypt, and Potiphar, **a eunuch of Pharaoh**, head of the executioners, an Egyptian man, buyeth him out of the hands of the Ishmaelites who have brought him thither.

Potiphar, an Egyptian eunuch, could legally marry in Egypt. In Israel or Judea and Judea, castrated eunuchs were forbidden to marry under Mosaic Law. So the fact that Potipher was a married eunuch supports the idea that he was a Born Eunuch.

Most individuals who were identified in the Bible as *saris* were not usually castrated slaves, but were, rather, appreciated, employed, and sometimes wealthy citizens who were gay.

> 1 Samuel 8:15 (written in Israel by Samuel) (YLT)
>
> And your seed and your vineyards he doth tithe, and hath given **to his eunuchs,** and to his servants

The eunuchs in the verse above were considered separately from servants so they were not servants or slaves. Here they could have been clerks, executives, or officers.

> 1 Kings 22:9 (written in Judah/Egypt by Jeremiah) (DRA)
>
> Then the king of Israel called **an eunuch,** and said to him: Make haste, and bring hither Micheas the son of Jemla.

> 2 Kings 8:6 (written in Judah/Egypt by Jeremiah) (YLT)
>
> And the king asketh at the woman, and she recounteth to him, and the king appointeth to her **a certain eunuch,** saying, 'Give back all that she hath, and all the increase of the field from the day of her leaving the land even till now.'

The eunuchs in these verses held a high rank and were trusted with important court business.

> 2 Kings 23:11 (written in Judah/Egypt by Jeremiah) (YLT)
>
> And he causeth to cease the horses that the kings of Judah have given to the sun from the entering in of the house of Jehovah, by the chamber **of Nathan-Melech the eunuch,** that is in the suburbs, and the chariots of the sun he hath burnt with fire.

In the above verse Jeremiah was describing a large upset with the kings of Judah involved with pagan idol worship that included animal sacrifice and fire. Jeremiah placed the event at a particular intersection, by the chamber of Nathan-Melech, an officer and eunuch in the employ of King Josiah, a Jewish king. Some have supposed that this eunuch was involved in taking care of the horses mentioned in the scripture but that is not actually stated by the author nor anywhere else. The eunuch, Nathan-Melech, could be named here because he was well known and his home would easily place the event at a known location. It would be like saying that there was a car wreck in front of Elton John's house.

2 Kings 24:12 (written in Judah/Egypt by Jeremiah) (YLT)

...and Jehoiachin king of Judah goeth out unto the king of Babylon, he, and his mother, and his servants, and his chiefs, **and his eunuchs**, and the king of Babylon taketh him in the eighth year of his reign...

2 Kings 24:15 (written in Judah/Egypt by Jeremiah) (YLT)

And he removeth Jehoiachin to Babylon, and the mother of the king, and the wives of the king, **and his eunuchs**, and the mighty ones of the land -- he hath caused a removal to go from Jerusalem to Babylon...

Jeremiah 29:2 (written in Judah/Egypt by Jeremiah) (ASV)

...after that Jeconiah the king, and the queen-mother, **and the eunuchs**, and the princes of Judah and Jerusalem, and the craftsmen, and the smiths, were departed from Jerusalem...

Jeremiah 34:19 (written in Judah/Egypt by Jeremiah) (KJV)

The princes of Judah, and the princes of Jerusalem, **the eunuchs**, and the priests, and all the people of the land, who passed between the parts of the calf;

Because these eunuchs in the above verses were in the employ of a Jewish king, they were Born Eunuchs. They had a status in the royal household, part of the immediate entourage of the royal family. There were many Born Eunuchs in the royal Jewish households in the Bible, all gay men.

In the King James Bible, the most reliable translation and the foundation for many contemporary translations, eunuchs were never identified as men, only as eunuchs or by their military title.

Born Eunuchs in the military in the times of the Bible.

There were many military eunuchs known by name in the scriptures. Sarsechim (prince of the eunuchs), was one of the generals of Nebuchadnezzar's army at the taking of Jerusalem (Jeremiah 39:3) and Nebushazban was an important officer (the Rab-saris, chief captain or "chief eunuch") of the Babylonian army, who with Nergal-sharezer and others were appointed to see to the safety of Jeremiah after the taking of Jerusalem (Jeremiah 39:13). These are Babylonian eunuchs.

However, in the verse below, the eunuch mentioned was in a responsible position in the military of Judah. As these are Jewish people, the eunuch mentioned here was not castrated, a practice which was banned by Jewish Law. Rather, this military officer had been serving a Jewish king, King Zedekiah, so he was a Born Eunuch:

> 2 Kings 25:19 and Jeremiah 52:25 (written in Judah/Egypt by Jeremiah) (YLT)
>
> ...and out of the city he hath taken **a certain eunuch** who is appointed over the men of war, and five men of those seeing the king's face who have been found in the city, and the head scribe of the host, who mustereth the people of the land, and sixty men of the people of the land who are found in the city,

As eunuchs had no families, no children, they were thought to be more loyal than straight men—not inclined to try and build their own empire and not likely to have conflicting allegiances — and so were trusted by rulers with important responsibilities, including military responsibilities. There were many gay military officers in the Bible, as noted here:

> 1 Chronicles 28:1 (written in Jerusalem by Ezra) (YLT)
>
> And David assembleth all the heads of Israel, heads of the tribes, and heads of the courses who are serving the king, and heads of the thousands, and heads of the hundreds, and heads of all the substance and possessions of the king, and of his sons, **with the officers (translated from saris) and the mighty ones, even to every mighty one of valour** -- unto Jerusalem.

2 Chronicles 18:8 (written in Jerusalem by Ezra) (KJV)

And the king of Israel called for one of his **officers (translated from the word saris)**, and said, Fetch quickly Micaiah the son of Imla.

How *Made Eunuchs* lived in the times of the Bible.

In the Book of Esther, the Bible story takes place in Persia so the eunuchs that cared for the King's women in this story are thought to be castrated. Here the word *saris* is repeatedly used in reference to officials in the palace of Ahasveros and refers to these persons being concerned with the care of the King's women. Because this was a Persian court and the Persian custom of the day was to have castrated eunuchs oversee the harems of the king's wives, we believe these were Made Eunuchs. These eunuchs are mentioned often in the story of Esther (Esther 1:10, Esther 1:12, Esther 1:15, Esther 2:3, Esther 2:14, Esther 2:15, Esther 4:4, Esther 4:5).

The eunuchs in the court of Ahasveros did everything for the concubines and wives of the King—all the beauty treatments and 'total makeovers' for the new ladies. Although Persian tradition would have these beauty and style professionals castrated, it is possible that there would be individuals that were drawn to this work, working with women in the beauty and fashion area. Also, the position of *eunuch* offered job security. Therefore some may have chosen the path of a Made Eunuch for that reason or were not castrated because they were Born Eunuchs, so it would be redundant to do so.

Eunuchs were also employed to guard the vestibule, the area between the outside world and the interior of the house. This gave the royal eunuch guards power as the literal gatekeepers to the King and his assets. It also was a position that was often corrupted by palace intrigue. Eunuchs not directly involved with the care of women were not necessarily castrated as castration involved additional financial compensation. So these eunuchs may have been Born Eunuchs.

Esther 2:21 (written by Mordecai in Shushan, Elam) (WEB)

In those days, while Mordecai was sitting in the king's gate, **two of the king's eunuchs**, Bigthan and Teresh, who were doorkeepers, were angry, and sought to lay hands on the King Ahasuerus.

Esther 6:2 (written by Mordecai in Shushan, Elam) (YLT)

...and it is found written that Mordecai had declared concerning Bigthana and Teresh, **two of the eunuchs of the king**, of the keepers of the threshold, who sought to put forth a hand on king Ahasuerus.

The story of Esther also included mention of other eunuchs in the King's household who were not employed in the care of women and so may have been Born Eunuchs, gay men:

Esther 6:14 (written by Mordecai in Shushan, Elam) (YLT)

They are yet speaking with him, and **eunuchs of the king** have come, and haste to bring in Haman unto the banquet that Esther hath made.

Esther 7:9 (written by Mordecai in Shushan, Elam) (NIV)

Then Harbona, **one of the eunuchs** attending the king, said, "A gallows seventy-five feet high stands by Haman's house. He had it made for Mordecai, who spoke up to help the king." The king said, "Hang him on it!"

Eunuchs have played important roles in the Bible.

As you read in the verse above, it was Harbona, one of the King's eunuchs, who made the timely suggestion to the king that resulted in the evil Haman to be hanged. Similarly, it was eunuchs, righteous gay men, who killed the evil Jezebel by throwing her out of a high window. It is understood that these heroes were Born Eunuchs as they were serving the daughter of a Jewish King. When Jehu entered the town of Jezreel, he heard Jezebel calling to him from a tower....

2 Kings 9:32-33 (written in Judah/Egypt by Jeremiah) (DRA)

And Jehu lifted up his face to the window, and said : Who is this? And **two or three eunuchs** bowed down to him. And he said to them: Throw her down headlong: and they threw her down, and the wall was sprinkled with her blood, and the hoofs of the horses trod upon her.

It was a eunuch who saved the prophet Jeremiah's life (Jeremiah 38:7 - 13). As this eunuch was a foreigner, it is possible that he was a Made Eunuch. His name means "slave king," so Ebed-melech might have been a captured royal. Here the prophet Jeremiah blessed this man and prophesied his victory over his enemies for his good deed.

It was a powerful eunuch, Ashpenaz, who was the one who consented to Daniel's request for a different diet than the diet the King ordered when Daniel and his friends were under house arrest in this foreign court. Daniel and his cousins were political prisoners in the court of Nebuchadnezzar in Babylon. In Babylon, castrated eunuchs were used to guard the female harem but eunuchs with other responsibilities were not necessarily castrated.

Because the scriptures also speak of the love between Daniel and Ashpenaz, it is quite likely that Ashpenaz was a Born Eunuch, a gay man, with a crush on Daniel. There are many translations about this relationship but the Bible says that the chief of the king's eunuchs, Ashpenaz, gave "tender love" (Daniel 1:9) to Daniel. The Hebrew word used here is *checed*, meaning *affectionate love*. The modern translations have watered this down significantly. *Checed* is used 250 times in the Old Testament and translated 174 times as *love*, but for some reason when referring to Ashpenaz's relationship to Daniel, the New International Version says *favor and sympathy*. Hmmm.

The last person Phillip baptized before the Lord translated him to Caesarea was a *saris*, a eunuch (Acts 8:27 - 39). As the sole representative of the Ethiopian monarch in Palestine, this person was obviously a very senior official, and there is no obvious reason to believe that he was a castrated eunuch (*Louw et al. 1993, vol. 1:107, 479, esp. n. 7, 482; vol. 2: 67, 109*). At the very least, it can be said that the type of eunuch this man was is not known but, since he was not a slave, it is quite likely he was a gay man.

God Gives a special blessing to eunuchs.

Most eunuchs in the Bible were Born Eunuchs, not castrated, or else they could not attend the temple. Castrated men were not permitted in the synagogue by Jewish Law (Deuteronomy 23:1; Leviticus 21:17; Leviticus 22:25). However, there were eunuchs in the Bible who were in the temple, therefore they were not castrated but were, rather, Born Eunuchs:

> Isaiah 56:3-5 (NLT)
>
> "Don't let foreigners who commit themselves to the LORD say, 'The LORD will never let me be part of his people.' And don't let **the eunuchs** say, 'I'm a dried-up tree with no children and no future.' For this is what the LORD says: **I will bless those eunuchs who keep my Sabbath days holy and who choose to do what pleases me and commit their lives to me. I will give them—within the walls of my house—a memorial and a name far greater than sons and daughters could give**. For the name I give them is an everlasting one. It will never disappear!

It is clear from the scriptures above that eunuchs were singled out by God for a blessing. Because this is a Jewish prophet's words, he was certainly referring to Born Eunuchs (gay men). Because the prophet also referred to foreigners in this blessing, he was including all outsiders in this insular Jewish community. God makes no distinctions as these are all people made by him, loved by him, and who all have a part to play in his plan for their lives. If the Bible authors were to re-draft their words today, it might read, "I will bless all my gay, lesbian, transgender, and bi-sexual children who love me—now and forever!"

**There was no law against sex
with eunuchs in Biblical times.**

In ancient times, in the time that both the Old and the New Testaments were written, there was no law by God or man against gay sex. The population we think of as "the gay male population" was considered by those who wrote the Bible as a third gender. This group was not considered male in a social or legal sense.

All the Biblical scriptures that today are used to condemn homosexuality were not written to condemn gay sex. These Biblical laws were all drafted to condemn male-on-male sex which was, by the most literal definition, hetero-sexual-on-heterosexual sexual abuse or ritualistic idol worship in some of the popular religions of the time. In the ancient world, all straight male-on-straight male sex was a practice of sexual humiliation, violent aggression, or social domination that straight men exercised upon one another or temple ritual sex (idol worship). This was illegal. However, in Biblical times, straight males could legally have sex with a passive non-male (eunuch or female). To not under-stand the ancient world's views in these gender issues renders the reader deaf and blind to God's Word in these areas.

The ancient world did not have any concept of lesbianism. In ancient times, when the Bible was written, there was no concept of a lesbian woman that con-forms to our contemporary concept of female homosexuality.

Jesus came to heal and yet Jesus never healed anyone from homosexuality or lesbianism. Jesus said the men born as eunuchs, who we today call gay men, should not marry women. Yet Jesus never condemned or spoke negatively about these Born Eunuchs.

We cannot understand the Bible unless we know what the writers are really say-ing. Here are all the books of the Bible in the order they were written and, here also, are the cultural annotations specific to the understanding these writers had of eunuchs in those times.

Pre-Bible

circa 2500 BC—The Sumero-Babylonia and Assyria culture considered there to be a gender that is not-male they called "a kulu'u," not a male. [*Ernst Weidner, "Aus den Tagen eines assyrischen Schattenkönigs," Archiv für Orientforschung, Vol. 10 No. 1 (1935), p. 3, p. 5, line 21*]

circa 2000 BC—the Pyramid Texts [*1462c*], possibly the oldest religious texts in the world, differentiate males from eunuchs, notes eunuchs as not male. [*Also noted Egyptologist, Kurt Sethe, states in his Work of this ancient time, "Die Aechtung feindlicher Fürsten, Völker und Dinge auf altägyptischen Tongefäßscherben des mittleren Reiches." in Abhandlungen der Preussischen Akademie der Wissenschaften (Proceedings of the Prussian Academy of Sciences), 1926, p.61, wherein eunuchs are classified separately from males and females.*]

circa 2000 BC – Earliest records for intentional human castration to create eunuchs are from the Sumerian city of Lagash (modern-day Iraq) [*Maekawa, Kazuya (1980). Animal and human castration in Sumer, Part II: Human castration in the Ur III period. Zinbun [Journal of the Research Institute for Humanistic Studies, Kyoto University], pp. 1–56.]; [Maekawa, Kazuya (1980). Female Weavers and Their Children in Lagash – Presargonic and Ur III. Acta Sumerologica 2:81–125.]* Castration is forbidden by Jewish Law so this only appears as a foreign practice.

Genesis | 1513 BC

Genesis 39:7 And it came to pass after these things, that his master's wife cast her eyes upon Joseph; and she said, Lie with me. (This passage refers to the fact that Potiphar, a eunuch, was married so he was most likely not castrated and, therefore, was a Born Eunuch in Genesis 37:36 and Genesis 39:1.)

Exodus | 1512 BC

Leviticus | 1512 BC

Leviticus 18:22 Thou shalt not lie with mankind, as with womankind: it is abomination. (Addressed to straight males and who, therefore, *would* lie with a woman. This law does not address sex with or between non-males, eunuchs.)

Leviticus 20:13 If a man also lie with mankind, as he lieth with a woman, both of them have committed an abomination: they shall surely be put to death; their blood shall be upon them. (A legally designated male is not to have sex with another legally designated male. This verse addresses only males and cannot include non-males, a third gender which would include all persons considered eunuchs by the author, Moses. This verse also does not forbid legal males from sex with non-males, such as eunuchs and women.)

Leviticus 22:24 Ye shall not offer unto the LORD that which is bruised, or crushed, or broken, or cut; neither shall ye make any offering thereof in your land. (Castrated animals are not fit for sacrificial offering to God. It is this verse that leads to the Jewish Law that forbids castrated males, Made Eunuchs, from entering the synagogue.)

Job | circa 1473 BC

Numbers | 1473 BC

Deuteronomy | 1473 BC

Deuteronomy 23:1 He that is wounded in the stones, or hath his privy member cut off, shall not enter into the congregation of the

LORD. (Castration of humans not permitted by Hebrew Law and castrated males not permitted in the synagogue.)

Joshua | circa 1450 BC

Judges | circa 1100 BC

Ruth | circa 1090 BC

1 Samuel | circa 1078 BC

2 Samuel | circa 1040 BC

Song of Solomon | circa 1020 BC

Ecclesiastes before 1000 BC

Jonah | circa 844 BC

Joel | circa 820 BC (?)

circa 850 – 622 BC—Made Eunuchs were familiar figures in the Assyrian Empire in the court of the Egyptian Pharaohs (down to the Lagid dynasty known as Ptolemies, ending with Cleopatra). [*Orlando Patterson, Slavery and Social Death, 511 pp., Harvard University Press, 1982 ISBN 0-674-81083-X, 9780674810839 (see p.315)*] However, this is not a Jewish practice, forbidden by Mosaic Law.

Amos | circa 804 BC

Hosea | after 745 BC

Isaiah | after 732 BC

Micah | before 717 BC

Proverbs | circa 717 BC

Zephaniah | before 648 BC

Nahum | before 632 BC

Habakkuk | circa 628 BC (?)

Lamentations | 607 BC

Obadiah | circa 607 BC

Ezekiel | circa 591 BC

> **circa 600 BC**—This era brings the first reports of males being castrated to change their gender so that more powerful males could have sex with them without consequence. This became customary in western Asia Minor in the early 6th century BC (*Herodotus III 48-49, 92. III 48*) but never in Jewish lands.

1 and 2 Kings | 580 BC

> **2 Kings 20:18** prophecy of Isaiah that Juda would be overthrown and the sons of the king made eunuchs, (since it was the custom to castrate slaves and prisoners of war in Mesopotamian countries where the practice probably started) (*Hug 1918:449-50; Grey 1974:580*)

Jeremiah | 580 BC

> **circa 550-350 BC**—Political eunuchism became a fully established institution among the Achamenide Persians (not the Jews). [*Orlando Patterson, Slavery and Social Death, 511 pp., Harvard University Press, 1982 ISBN 0-674-81083-X, 9780674810839 (see p.315)*]

Daniel | circa 536 BC

Haggai | 520 BC

Zechariah | 518 BC

Esther | circa 475BC

1 and 2 Chronicles | circa 460 BC

Ezra | circa 460 BC

Psalms | circa 460 BC

Nehemiah | after 443 BC

Malachi | after 443BC

circa 360 BC—Aristole publishes his work "Generation of Animals IV 1", stating that a eunuch is neither male nor female so is a third gender. Many Jewish Biblical authors are educated men exposed to the teachings and influences of Aristole in addition to their own understanding of gender of those times that classified male, female, and 'other.'

circa 200-300 BC—Many Eunuchs are considered safer than uncastrated eunuchs as the later may be pretending to be a Born Eunuchs to gain access to women and household assets. [*Refer to the comic plays by Menander (circa 343-291 BC) and Terence (circa 195 – 159 BC) about men pretending to be born eunuchs and texts from the Wisdom of Sirach, 20:4, (circa 200 -175 BC)]*

Matthew | circa 41 AD

circa 10 AD—Roman culture of the time considers born eunuchs a neutral gender [*Ovid, Amores, II 3.5-6]*, neither male nor female.

Matthew 19:12 Jesus's words about eunuchs was spoken during his life but not documented until four decades later. Here Jesus says there are Born Eunuchs, Made Eunuchs and Self-Made Eunuchs, of which he is one. Since Jesus did not castrate himself, he is not speaking of anything physical. The word Jesus chose was *saris*, an Aramaic word which was translated into Hebrew as *eunuch* and translated into Greek as *eunouchos* in this verse and is also understood to mean virgin. *Saris* are not considered male and this was understood by the ancient people of those times. They were considered a third gender. [Hester, J. David (2005). "Eunuchs and the Postgender Jesus: Matthew 19:12 and Transgressive Sexualities"(PDF). *Journal for the Study of the New Testament.* **28** (1): 13-40. doi: 10.1177/0142064X05057772. Retrieved 2 April 2011]

1 Thessalonians | circa 50 AD

2 Thessalonians | circa 51 AD

Galatians | circa 50-52 AD

1 Corinthians | circa 55 AD

1 Corinthians 6:9—Paul wrote to the Corinth church in Greece to decry the common Greek practice of straight men having sexual intercourse with other straight men as a show of superiority and masculinity over those younger or of lesser social rank. This was also routinely practiced in the Greek military where it was encouraged by the State. [Victor David Hanson, *The Western Way of War: Infantry Battle in Classical Greece* (University of California Press, 1994, 2009), p. 124.]

2 Corinthians | circa 55 AD

Romans | circa 56 AD

Luke | circa 56-58 AD

Ephesians | circa 60-61 AD

circa 60 AD—Despot Roman Emperor Nero castrated a young boy so that he could then legally marry him [*C. Suetonius Tranquillus, the Life of Nero, 28]*

Colossians | circa 60-61 AD

Philemon | circa 60-61 AD

Philippians | circa 60-61 AD

Hebrews | circa 61 AD

Acts | circa 61 AD

James | before 62 AD

Mark | circa 60-65 AD

1 Timothy | circa 61-64 AD

> **1 Timothy 1:9-10**—Paul wrote to his fellow Turk, Timothy, who had recently worked with him in Greece, and labeled as sin the common Greek practice of straight men sexually engaging with other straight men. [Plato, Phaedrus in the *Symposium*]

Titus | circa 61-64 AD

1 Peter | circa 62-64 AD

2 Peter | circa 64 AD

2 Timothy | circa 65 AD

Jude | circa 65 AD

Revelation | circa 96 AD

> **circa 85 AD**—Domitian, Roman Emperor, decreed a law that forbade anyone within Roman jurisdiction to geld a boy. [*Ammianus Marcellinus XVIII 4.5 Suetonius, Domitian, 7] [See also Martial IX 8.5-6.*] I am guessing Nero's little stunt 25 years prior shocked the authorities.

John | circa 98 AD

1 John | circa 98 AD

2 John | circa 98 AD

3 John | circa 98 AD

circa 120 AD—Hadrian, Roman Emperor 117-138 AD, levied penalties for castration. [Ulpian *Lex Julia et Papia, Book 1* (D 48.8.4.2)]

circa 360 AD—Gregory of Nazianzus, 4th-century Archbishop of Constantinople, a Doctor of the Catholic Church, and one of the three Holy Hierarchs in Eastern Catholic Churches warned Born Eunuchs to not be arrogant about their sexual abstinence (with women), thinking it makes them more spiritual, and also warning them against partaking in ritual prostitution, a traditional practice of eunuchs since Babylonian times (*Oration 37:16-17*).

circa 400 AD—Catholic Church redefines eunuchs as males and prosecutes them as sodomites [Rev. M. Hyamson, ed. and tr., *Mosaicarum et romanarum legum collatio*, London, 1913 (reprint Buffalo, 1997), pp. 82-83. (Coll. leg. mos. et rom. 5.3.1-2) and Epiphanius of Salamis, *Basket of Heresies*, 4.3.2-5].

Here the Catholic Church borrowed a word from the Bible, *sodomite*, that had heretofore only referred to male temple prostitutes—those who engaged in sexual depravity as idol worshipers—and illogically applied it to all eunuchs, both Born Eunuchs and Made Eunuchs.

circa 540 AD—Byzantine Emperor Justinian levies penalties for castration and recognizes eunuchs as a special category of men. [*New Constitutions of Justinian*, 77 and 141. Authority for dates is the work of Derrick Sherwin Bailey, *Homosexuality and the Western Christian Tradition*, London, 1955 (reprint 1975), pp. 73ff.]

circa 600 AD—Salic Law of the Franks levy penalties for castration (*Lex Salica XXIX 7*)

Certain excerpts used here with permission from researcher Faris Malik http://www.well. com/user/aquarius/egypt.htm; http://www.well.com/user/aquarius/cardiff.htm; http://www. well.com/user/aquarius/rome.htm

The timeline above shows that in the era of the Bible's authors, eunuchs were not male and were not referenced in any scripture as male.

However, three hundred years after the last book in the Bible was written, in 400AD, the Catholic Church decided to redefine eunuchs as males and to prosecute them as sodomites, the term that had been used in the Bible exclusively for male temple prostitutes who partake in ritualistic sex worship.

This is the point in time where the Church changed the meaning of scriptural terms the Bible authors had used throughout the Old and New Testaments and thus invented an entirely new bigotry, homophobia. [Rev. M. Hyamson, ed. and tr., *Mosaicarum et romanarum legum collatio*, London, 1913 (reprint Buffalo, 1997), pp. 82-83. (Coll. leg. mos. et rom. 5.3.1-2) and Epiphanius of Salamis, *Basket of Heresies*, 4.3.2-5]

We must understand the language of Biblical times.

It is illuminating to know exactly what the Bible authors meant by the word *eunuch*. It is also important to know what the term *High Priest* meant, what the role of the High Priest was in Biblical times, because the Bible states that Jesus is our High Priest.

Wherefore in all things it behoved him to be made like unto his brethren, that he might be a merciful and faithful **high priest** in things pertaining to God, to make reconciliation for the sins of the people.

Hebrews 4:14 (KJV)

Seeing then that we have a great **high priest**, that is passed into the heavens, Jesus the Son of God, let us hold fast our profession.

The sins of the High Priest were regarded as the sins of the people (Leviticus 4:3,22). In antiquity, the High Priest was either good or bad and God judged the entire nation based on whether their High Priest and his annual offering in the Holy of Holies was acceptable.

So when the Bible says Jesus is our High Priest, that means it is not us that must be acceptable to God, but it is *Jesus Christ* as our High Priest who must be acceptable to God. So it is not you being judged by God. It is Jesus who is being judged by God.

1 John 4:17 (KJV)

Herein is our love made perfect, that we may have boldness in the day of judgment: **because as he is, so are we in this world**.

As God finds Jesus, so he finds us in this world. That means on Earth now, not in Heaven later. Is Jesus acceptable to God? Yes. So we are to keep our eyes off ourselves. We are only to put our eyes on Jesus. So does it matter who is gay or straight? No. It only matters who is Jesus.

We are told to make an effort to understand the Bible.

We were made to know and understand the Bible. We were not made to be ignorant. In John 8:31 - 32, Jesus put it this way: "If ye continue in my word, then are ye my disciples indeed; and ye shall know the truth, and the truth shall make you free." (KJV)

Nothing in the Bible is to be a secret from us.

> Luke 8:10 (KJV)
>
> And he said, Unto you it is given to know the mysteries of the kingdom of God: but to **others** in parables; that seeing they might not see, and hearing they might not understand.

We are not the *others* referenced in the above scripture. We are his beloved, his Church, and it is to us that the Bible is to be totally known and understood as the rock of truth that it is. So if every Christian knew what you just learned about what the Bible really says about the gay issue, would that change the church you attend?

Love - Proof 4

Love is proof that any problems traditional Church teachings have with homosexuality are based on lies.

The word *love* has been kicked around and used as an excuse for wife beating, spanking children, and even murder. There are four Hebrew words in the Old Testament and three Greek words in the New Testament that were all translated into the single English word *love* in our American Bibles. It sounds as if it could be confusing to know exactly what is love with multiple terms and multiple expressions and outcomes from love.

We are ordered by God to love.

From the Old Testament through the New Testament, from Genesis through Revelation, it is clear that God is love, love made the world, and we're designed by God to love each other in this world. A baby loves its parents, parents love their children, people love their country and flowers and lasagna. But loving each other is a mandate from God.

John 15:12 (the words of Jesus) (NRSV)

This is my commandment, that **you love one another**, as I have loved you.

John 15:9 (the words of Jesus) (KJV)

As the Father hath loved me, so have I loved you: **continue ye in my love**.

Ephesians 4:1-3 (NRSV)

I therefore, the prisoner in the Lord, beg you to lead a life worthy of the calling to which you have been called, with all humility and gentleness, with patience, bearing with **one another in love**, making every effort to maintain the unity of the Spirit in the bond of peace.

1 John 3:23-24 (NRSV)

And this is his commandment, that we should believe in the name of his Son Jesus Christ **and love one another**, just as he has commanded us. All who obey his commandments abide in him, and he abides in them. And by this we know that he abides in us, by the Spirit that he has given us.

Romans 13:8 (NKJV)

Owe no one anything except **to love one another**, for **he who loves another has fulfilled the law**.

We owe each other love. "One another" means everyone. We owe it to God to love the boss, the politician, the child, the neighbor. There are no exceptions. Therefore the Bible also says that we owe it to God to love the gay boss, the gay politician, the gay child, the gay neighbor. There are no exceptions. The Bible doesn't say, "Except for..."

2 John 1: 5-6 (NRSV)

And now I plead with you, lady, not as though I wrote a new commandment to you, but that which we have had from the beginning: **that we love one another**. This is love, that we walk according to His commandments. This is the commandment, that as you have heard **from the beginning**, you should walk in it.

So we have been commanded by God from the beginning to love one another. *From the beginning* means before there were the Ten Commandments. So *love* was the overarching commandment from God before Moses, from the beginning of the world, the commandment that covers the Ten Commandments.

Jesus explains how the Ten Commandments are reduced to Two Commandments.

The Ten Commandments were given to Moses by God and recorded in Exodus 20:1 - 17 and these Ten Commandments were repeated by Moses again, almost word-for-word, in Deuteronomy 5:6 - 21.

Deuteronomy 5:6-22 (NRSV)

(1) I am the Lord your God, who brought you out of the land of Egypt, out of the house of slavery; you shall have no other gods before me.

(2) You shall not make for yourself an idol, whether in the form of anything that is in heaven above, or that is on the Earth beneath, or that is in the water under the earth. You shall not bow down to them or worship them; for I am the Lord your God am a jealous God, punishing children for the iniquity of parents, to the third and fourth generation of those who reject me, but showing steadfast love to the thousandth generation of those who love me and keep my Commandments.

(3) You shall not make wrongful use of the name of the Lord your God, for the Lord will not acquit anyone who misuses his name.

(4) Observe the Sabbath day and keep it holy, as the Lord your God commanded you. Six days you shall labor and do all of your work. But the seventh day is the Sabbath to the Lord your God; you shall not do any work - you, or your son or your daughter, or your male or female slave, or your ox or donkey, or any of your livestock, or the resident alien in your towns, so that your male and female slave may rest as well as you. Remember that you were a slave in the land of Egypt,

and the Lord your God brought you out from there with a mighty hand and an outstretched arm; therefore the Lord your God commanded you to keep the Sabbath day.

(**5**) Honor your father and your mother, as the Lord your God commanded you, so that your days may be long and that it may go well with you in the land that the Lord your God is giving you.

(**6**) You shall not murder.

(**7**) Neither shall you commit adultery.

(**8**) Neither shall ye steal.

(**9**)Neither shall you bear false witness against your neighbor.

(**10**)Neither shall you covet your neighbor's wife. Neither shall ye desire your neighbor's house, or field, or male or female slave, or ox, or donkey, or anything that belongs to your neighbor.

In the Ten Commandments there is no commandment that forbids gay relationships. In fact, the Ten Commandments and the verse immediately following the Ten Commandments in Deuteronomy make it clear that this was the entire list of that heavenly mandate and there are no more:

Deuteronomy 5:22 (NRSV)

These words the Lord spoke with a loud voice to your whole assembly at the mountain, out of the fire, the cloud, and the thick darkness, **and he added no more**. He wrote them on two stone tablets, and gave them to me.

As few and simple as these ten rules are, Jesus further clarified God's commandments by boiling the entire list down to two Commandments in the story of an exchange between Jesus and the Pharisee lawyer that is told three times, in Matthew, Mark, and in Luke.

Matthew 22:34-40 (NRSV)

When the Pharisees heard that he [Jesus] had silenced the Sadducees, they gathered together, and one of them, a lawyer, asked him a question to test him. "Teacher, which command-ment in the law is the greatest?" He said to him, "'You shall love the Lord your God with all your heart, and with all your soul, and with all your mind'. This is the greatest and first commandment. And the second is like it: 'You shall love your neighbor as yourself.' **On these two commandments hang all the law and the prophets.**"

In this scripture, *the law* here refers to the Ten Commandments as well as the many other laws in the scriptures. So Jesus is stating that the Ten Commandments and all the other laws in the Old Testament are summed up in these two Commandments: Love God, and Love All Others.

Mark 12:28-34 (NRSV)

One of the scribes came near and heard them disputing with one another, and seeing that he answered them well, he asked them, "Which commandment is the first of all?" Jesus answered, "The first is, 'Hear, O Israel: the Lord our God, the Lord is one; you shall love the Lord your God with all your heart, and with all your soul, and with all your mind, and with all your strength, the second is this, **you shall love your neigh-bor as yourself**.' There is no other commandment greater than these." Then the scribes said to him, "You are right, Teacher; you have truly said that **'he is one, and besides him there is no other;' and 'to love him with all the heart, and with all the understanding, and with all the strength,' and 'to love one's neighbor as one's self,' – this is much more important than all whole burnt offerings and sacrifices."** When Jesus saw that he answered wisely, he said to him, "You are not far from the kingdom of God." After that no one dared to ask him any question.

In those days believers would give to the synagogue cash, grain, animals, and other valuables as sacrifices to atone for all their known or unknown trans-gressions against the law. But here the scribe speaking to Jesus states that the practice of these two Commandments of Love is superior to the practice of ritual sacrifice. So if ritual sacrifice was a practice designed to blot out sin, the practice of love is superior, more effective, at blotting out sin than the practice of sacrifice and giving offerings.

Luke 10:25-28 (NRSV)

Just then a lawyer stood up to test Jesus. "Teacher," he said, "what must I do to inherit eternal life?" He said to him, "What is written in the law? What do you read there?" He answered, **"You shall love the Lord your God with all your heart, and with all your soul, and with all your strength, and with all your mind; and your neighbor as yourself**." And he said to him, "You have given the right answer; do this, and you will live."

This Commandment Jesus is referring to is a quote from Moses, what Moses said after he wrote down the Ten Commandments for the second time. After the Ten Commandments are recorded in Deuteronomy Chapter 5, Moses says in Chapter 6:

Deuteronomy 6:1-5 (NKJV)

Now this is the commandment, and these are the statutes and judgments which the Lord your God has commanded to teach you, that you may observe them in the land which you are crossing over to possess, that you may fear the Lord your God, to keep all his statutes and his Commandments which I command you, you and your son and your grandson all the days of your life, and that your days may be prolonged. Therefore hear, O Israel, and be careful to observe it, that it may be well with you, and that you may multiply greatly as the Lord God of your fathers had promised you – 'a land flowing with milk and honey.' **Hear, O Israel: the Lord our God, the Lord is one! You shall love the Lord your God with all your heart, with all your soul, and with all your strength**.

Moses is taking what we consider the first four Commandments of the ten and expressing what they mean. God did not give the Commandments to Moses as a list of ten rules. The Ten Commandments are not numbered in the Bible.

That is a later invention. So these commandments were all expressed by God all together. And what we consider the first four are about loving God:

-Have no other gods but God,
-Do not worship idols,
-Do not misuse his name, and
-Observe the Sabbath

These are all the ways we are to express our love for God and to love him completely with everything we have—our words, our time, our thoughts. If you love God, you will have no other gods, you will not use his name as a curse word, and you will routinely set aside time in your schedule to study his Word, pray and reflect on him.

So where did the second commandment come from? There is no "Love your neighbor as yourself" in the Ten Commandments.

The second commandment Jesus is quoting in Matthew and Mark is from Leviticus, written after Moses brought the Ten Commandments down from the mountain.

Leviticus 19:18 (NIV)

Do not seek revenge or bear a grudge against anyone among your people, **but love your neighbor as yourself**. I am the LORD.

Elsewhere in Leviticus, Moses has greatly enlarged the minimalist, original Ten Commandments but they have all been drafted by him with the overarching requirement that these laws be the expression of love and respect toward one another.

So, regard the final six Commandments of the Ten that are about loving others:

-Honor your parents,
-Don't murder,
-Don't commit adultery,

-Don't steal,

-Don't lie about someone, and

-Don't want their stuff.

All of these Commandments are ways to express the idea of love and respect for others. If you loved and respected others, you would not murder them, lie about them, steal their stuff or even want their stuff, nor would you mess up their marriage. All these ideas can be boiled down to one overarching commandment: "Love one another." This is what Moses was communicating—that all the rules and laws that concern how we treat each other are all an expression of a prime mandate from God to love one another. So love is not necessarily a feeling. It is how we treat each other in concrete ways.

If the first Commandment is to love God, then we must also love God's creation that he loves. So the first and second commandment—love God and love one another—are really two sides of the same coin. We must love each other if we love God:

1 John 4:20-21 (NRSV)

Those who say, "I love God," and hate their brothers or sisters, are liars; for those who do not love a brother or sister whom they have seen, cannot love God whom they have not seen. The commandment we have from him is this: those who love God must love their brothers and sisters also.

So the Ten Commandments have become the Two Commandments that have become the One Commandment. And the One (and only) Commandment of Love includes us all:

Psalm 119:96 (NRSV)

I have seen a limit to a perfection, but **your commandment is exceedingly broad**.

The Commandment of Love applies broadly—it broadly applies to those who are commanded to love others so that's all of us. No one is excluded. And the

Commandment of Love broadly applies to those we are commanded to love. So that's everyone. No one is disqualified from being loved by you—gay or straight.

God is love.

Why would God give us all only *one thing* to do—to love? Why? . That is all he is. So that is why he has summed it up in this one concept — love.

> 1 John 4:7-17 (NKJV)
>
> Beloved, let us love one another, for **love is of God**; and everyone who loves is born of God and knows God. He who does not love does not know God, for **God is love**. In this the love of God was manifested toward us, that God has sent His only begotten Son into the world, that we might live through Him. In this is love, not that we loved God, but that **He loved us** and sent His Son *to be* the propitiation for our sins. Beloved, if **God so loved us**, we also ought to love one another. No one has seen God at any time. If we love one another, God abides in us, and His love has been perfected in us. By this we know that we abide in Him, and He in us, because He has given us of His Spirit. And we have seen and testify that the Father has sent the Son *as* Savior of the world. Whoever confesses that Jesus is the Son of God, God abides in him, and he in God. And we have known and believed the love that God has for us. **God is love**, and he who abides in love abides in God, and God in him. Love has been perfected among us in this: that we may have boldness in the day of judgment; **because as He is, so are we in this world**.

Did you catch that last bit? "As he is, so are we in this world." The *he* in that verse is Jesus. As Jesus is in Heaven, so are we in this world. That's how God loves us—just like he loves Jesus.

So if God is love, what does that mean to us?

Psalm 145:8-9 (NKJV)

The Lord is gracious, and full of compassion; slow to anger, and of great mercy. **The Lord is good to all**: and his tender mercies *are* over all his works.

This is the picture of love in action, God in action: full of compassion, slow to anger and merciful.

1 Corinthians 13:1-8 (NKJV)

Though I speak with the tongues of men and of angels, but have not love, I have become sounding brass or a clanging cymbal. And though I have *the gift* of prophecy, and understand all mysteries and all knowledge, and though I have all faith, so that I could remove mountains, but have not love, I am nothing. And though I bestow all my goods to feed *the poor,* and though I give my body to be burned, but have not love, it profits me nothing. Love suffers long *and* is kind; love does not envy; love does not parade itself, is not puffed up; does not behave rudely, does not seek its own, is not provoked, thinks no evil; does not rejoice in iniquity, but rejoices in the truth; **bears all things, believes all things, hopes all things, endures all things. Love never fails.** But whether there are prophecies, they will fail; whether there are tongues, they will cease; whether there is knowledge, it will vanish away.

Since God is love, you can replace the word *love* in the above verses with the word *God* and learn more about God's heart and nature: God suffers long and is kind; God does not envy; God does not parade himself, God is not puffed up; God does not behave rudely, God thinks no evil; God does not rejoice in iniquity (bad things), but God rejoices in the truth; God bears all things, God endures all things. God never fails.

Jesus is love.

I read about a man who had trouble with the idea that God sent Jesus to Earth as a man and that Jesus was the man-version of God. This man's thinking was, if God is God, why would he need to ever have his son be on Earth as a man?

What was the point? He was God. He didn't need a human (lesser) version of himself.

One day the man was endeavoring to move his flock of geese into the barn. There was a storm coming and the geese would not be able to withstand the storm if they were not moved to shelter. So the man opened wide the barn door and proceeded to try and herd the birds toward the barn. But the geese would scatter instead.

As the storm was approaching the man tried harder with no success as the geese became more agitated and would not enter the barn. They would not listen to the man. They would not respond to his waving arms the way he hoped they would respond.

Then the man got an idea. He ran and got his own pet goose that he kept near the house. This goose was tame and understood the movements of the man. The man put his pet goose in the midst of the flock and then he called out to the pet goose to follow him into the barn. The pet goose followed the man into the barn and the rest of the geese followed the pet goose into the barn also.

Then the man had a revelation that this is why God had to send a man to Earth, even though he was God. God needed a man on Earth who knew him, and who would hear him, so that other men on Earth would know God themselves through the example of God's man.

God had Jesus in place before the foundation of the world to represent him to us here on Earth so we would know him.

John 1:1 (KJV)

In the beginning was the Word, and the Word was with God, and the Word was God.

John 1:14 (KJV)

And the Word was made flesh, and dwelt among us, (and we beheld his glory, the glory as of the only begotten of the Father,) full of grace and truth.

Before Christ, men on Earth were missing it. Translators garbled the Ancient Hebrew permissive tense and that is why there is so much in the Old Testament about God raining down curses on men, punishing and killing those who sin. Because the English language has no corresponding permissive tense, if you just read the Old Testament as it is commonly translated, you would get the idea that God is a mean Daddy indeed. The world needed Jesus to show us and teach us the truth about God and the world and that God is love. There is a huge and measurable difference in the Old and New Testaments relative to the word *love*.

John 14:9 (KJV)

Jesus saith unto him, Have I been so long time with you, and yet hast thou not known me, Philip? **he that hath seen me hath seen the Father**; and how sayest thou then, Show us the Father?

The New Testament shows God's loving heart.

According to Strong's, the word *love* appears 131 times in the Old Testament and 179 times in the New Testament. However, the Old Testament is a considerably longer text than the New Testament. In one printed version of the Bible, the Old Testament covers 928 pages and the New Testament, comparatively smaller, covers only 246 pages. That means, measuring by density—*mentions* relative to the number of *pages*—the word *love* appears in the New Testament 5.15 times more than in the Old Testament. The New Testament is the document that reveals God's new covenant with us and shows us more clearly God's love for us through Jesus.

God needed Jesus to show us love. God needed Jesus to take the temple ritual that man had used to interact with God and show it as only the rehearsal that it was and replace it with the real thing — love. No more sacrifices — because Jesus becomes the final sacrificial lamb. No more trying to be perfect — because Jesus becomes our High Priest and only he needs to be perfect. No more needing intermediaries to speak to God. At Jesus' last gasp on the cross, the curtains in the temple tore open, top to bottom, and the Holy Spirit left the temple and now dwells in the temple of our bodies. God is no more in temples of stone.

> Luke 9:55-56 (Jesus' words) (KJV)
>
> But he turned, and rebuked them, and said, "Ye know not what manner of spirit ye are of. **For the Son of man is not come to destroy men's lives, but to save them."**

After Jesus came and lived and taught, even though it was brief, his teachings have vibrated throughout the entire world, changing the hearts of people, moving governments and nations, all through the doctrine of love.

> Ephesians 3:14-19 (KJV)
>
> For this cause I bow my knees unto the Father of our Lord Jesus Christ, of whom the whole family in heaven and earth is named, that he would grant you, according to the riches of his glory, to be strengthened with might by his Spirit in the inner man; that Christ may dwell in your hearts by faith; that ye, **being rooted and grounded in love**, may be able to comprehend with all saints what is the breadth, and length, and depth, and height; and to know **the love of Christ**, which passeth knowledge, that ye might be filled with all the fullness of God.

So what would Jesus do?

Sounds like a joke—WWJD. But it is a great test for everything including how we treat each other. So if you don't know how to show love, ask yourself WWJD. Would Jesus rebuke the gay couple? He never did. Would Jesus "pray away the gay?" He never even thought about it. Would Jesus condemn a person for being gay? Never.

What did he do? He loved everyone and commanded us to follow him and do the same.

Love

.7276

mentions per page

...so although there are only slightly more mentions of love in the New Testament, the density of the mentions in the New Testament is more than 5 times that of the Old Testament.

.144

mentions per page

The Old Testament is a much larger collection of books than the New Testament. Based on a typical printing, the Old Testament is 337.24% larger than the New Testament

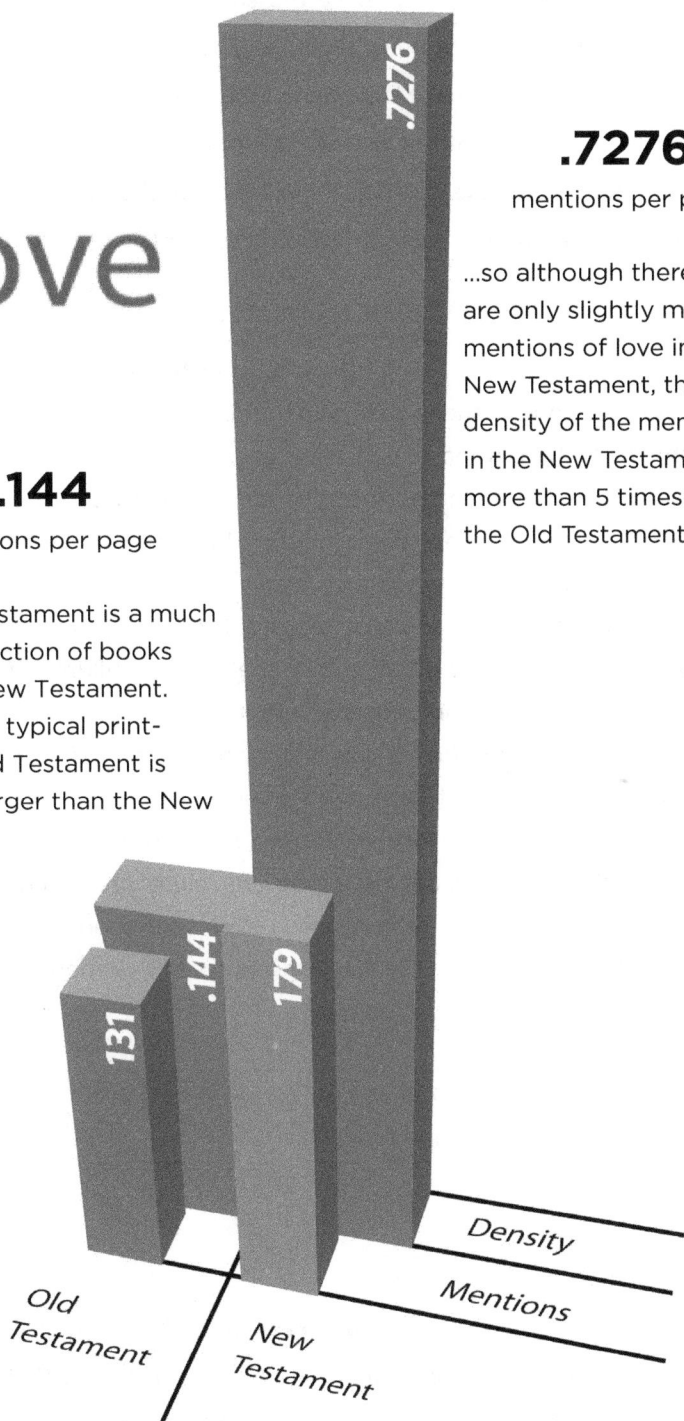

.7276

131

.144

179

Density

Mentions

Old Testament

New Testament

Have you heard that statement: "Love the sinner, hate the sin?" These two ideas are both in the Bible but never together. There are two things wrong with linking these two ideas into one statement. ONE: This statement is commonly aimed at homosexuals. But homosexuality is not a sin. TWO: If the *sin* referred to was an actual sin, such as murder, then if we love the murderer, we are not seeing the sin at all. We only see our beloved brother (or sister).

> Luke 6:32-38 (the words of Jesus) (KJV)
>
> For if ye love them which love you, what thank have ye? For sinners also love those that love them. And if ye do good to them which do good to you, what thank have ye? For sinners also do even the same. And if ye lend to them of whom ye hope to receive, what thank have ye? For sinners also lend to sinners, to receive as much again. But love ye your enemies, and do good, and lend, hoping for nothing again; and your reward shall be great, and ye shall be the children of the Highest: for he is kind unto the unthankful and to the evil. **Be ye therefore merciful**, as your Father also is merciful. **Judge not**, and ye shall not be judged: **condemn not**, and ye shall not be condemned: **forgive**, and ye shall be forgiven: **give**, and it shall be given unto you; good measure, pressed down, and shaken together, and running over, shall men give into your bosom. For with the same measure that ye mete withal it shall be measured to you again.

Jesus says we are to condemn not and judge not. What part of Christ's directive here permits us to condemn and judge?

You are love.

Remember that as Jesus is (in Heaven) so are we in this world. Remember that Jesus is love. So that means we are love, too! Can we live up to that? It is in our DNA. We are love. We were designed that way from the foundation of the world!

Ephesians 4:31-32; 5:1-2 (NRSV)

Put away from you all bitterness and wrath and anger and wrangling and slander, together with all malice, and **be kind to one another, tenderhearted, forgiving one another, as God in Christ has forgiven you.** ... Therefore be imitators of God, as beloved children, and live in love, as Christ loved us and gave himself up for us, a fragrant offering and sacrifice to God.

Christians who are not behaving with love are not following Christ.

Jonathan and David are the embodiment of love in the Bible.

From what we read in the Bible, Jonathan only just saw David for the first time that famous day, the day David slew Goliath, the day David made his reputation as a giant-killer. There is no text that records any conversation between David and Jonathan on that day and yet, after David's successful slaying of the enemy giant, just after Saul approached David to inquire whose son he was, then the Bible says that the two young men, David and Jonathan, were in love.

1 Samuel 18:1-4 (NRSV)

When David had finished speaking to Saul, the soul of Jonathan was bound to the soul of David, and Jonathan loved him as his own soul. Saul took him that day and would not let him return to his father's house. Then Jonathan made a covenant with David, because he loved him as his own soul. Jonathan stripped himself of the robe that he was wearing, and gave it to David, and his armor, and even his sword and his bow and his belt.

Later King Saul grew jealous of David and planned to have the young man killed, so Jonathan vowed to be faithful to David rather than to his own father and to help David in any way he could to escape.

1 Samuel 20:16-17 (NRSV)

Thus **Jonathan made a covenant with the house of David**, saying, "May the Lord seek out the enemies of David." Jonathan made David swear again by his love for him; for he loved him as he loved his own life.

Jonathan's father did not approve of his son aligning himself with David against him. Saul even suggested that the relationship between the two young men was inappropriate.

1 Samuel 20:30 (NRSV)

Then Saul's anger was kindled against Jonathan. He said to him, "You son of a perverse, rebellious woman! **Do I not know that you had chosen the son of Jesse to your own shame**, and to the shame of your mother's nakedness?"

When it was clear that the King was indeed seeking the death of David, Jonathan and David had a tearful parting, never to see each other again:

1 Samuel 20:42 (NRSV)

Then Jonathan said to David, "**Go in peace, since both of us have sworn the name of the Lord, saying, 'The Lord shall be between me and you, and between my descendants and your descendants, forever.'**" He got up and left: and Jonathan went into the city.

From the scripture above, they both clearly planned on fathering children one day. It is not necessary that these two men be gay to explain this love they had for each other. But it is very important that the Bible has carefully recorded their bond, their affection, and their love for each other as being one that "surpasses the love of women."

2 Samuel 1:26 (NRSV)

I am distressed for you, my brother Jonathan; **greatly beloved were you to me; your love to me was wonderful, passing the love of women**.

Does the Bible mean that this love surpasses the love of women in general, meaning that the love between David and Jonathan was superior in quality to what is understood as the romantic love that straight men feel toward their female partner?

Was this love bond more respectable than a love bond between a man and a woman since women were little more than property in those days?

Going forward, there is no other mention in the Bible of either David or Jonathan having any affection for another man in their future lives and there is considerable documentation that David had a great sexual interest in women and took serious risks to consummate his sexual lust for women. Since David was King, he would not have to fake this to impress anyone.

And even though Jonathan died young in battle, he still left offspring. So he wasn't resisting female relationships.

What the Bible describes in the story of David and Jonathan is two straight men who are totally devoted to each other, loved each other, and it was clear that nothing could ever break that connection these two had together. It is perfect scriptural love—not petty, boastful, or fleeting. It is forever love, real love.

And the fact that this love is between two men—that the Bible does not choose to depict perfect love through the example of a man and a woman—communicates that real love, perfect love, is not defined by gender. Real love is not defined by sexual orientation. Real love is how God loves us. And God made us able to have real love with the same sex as well as the opposite sex. Homophobia is the idea that real love between opposite sex partners is superior to real love between same sex partners. This conceit is not supported by the Bible.

The real Christian walk is love.

There are many churches and whole denominations that teach the false doctrine of a God who only made heterosexuality. This is false doctrine not supported in the Bible. The sexuality issue is an obsession of carnal mankind, not God's.

Isaiah 55:8-9 (NRSV)

For my thoughts are not your thoughts, nor are your ways my ways, says the LORD. For as the heavens are higher than the earth, so **are my ways higher than your ways and my thoughts than your thoughts**.

God's thoughts are one single commandment—love. And if we keep this one commandment, we are proving that we love God and all whom God loves.

1 John 5:1-3 (NKJV)

Whoever believes that Jesus is the Christ is born of God, and everyone who loves Him who begot also loves him who is begotten of Him. By this we know that we love the children of God, when we love God and keep His commandments. For this is the love of God, that we keep his commandments. And his commandments are not burdensome.

It is easier to love than otherwise. How do you feel when you hate? Not good. Who do you love? If we do the right thing, we love everyone. God loves everyone. Do you think your mother loved you? Maybe she did and maybe she didn't. But God is perfect so he loves you. He has your face drawn on the palms of his hands. He can hold his hands up and see you right there anytime he wants to smile. It's as if God takes out his wallet just to look at your picture he keeps there.

Isaiah 49:15-16 (NRSV)

Can a woman forget her nursing child, or show no compassion for the child of her womb? Even these may forget, yet I will not forget you. **See, I have inscribed you on the palms of my hands**; your walls are continually before me.

Does God say "I have inscribed you on the palms of my hands—unless you're gay."? No.

> 1 John 2:8-11 (NRSV)
>
> Yet I am writing you a new commandment that it's true in him and in you, because the darkness is passing away and the true light is already shining. **Whoever says, "I am in the light," while hating a brother or sister, is still in the darkness**. Whoever loves a brother or sister lives in the light, and in such a person there is no cause for stumbling. But whoever hates another believer is in the darkness, walks in the darkness, and does not know the way to go, because the darkness has brought on blindness.

Anyone who judges, criticizes, hates, shuns or does not love their gay brother or sister in Christ is walking in darkness.

> James 2:8-9 (NRSV)
>
> You do well if you really fulfill the royal law according to the Scripture, **"You shall love your neighbor as yourself." But if you show partiality**, you commit sin and are convicted by the law as transgressors.

Let's restate this scripture correctly: "You shall love your gay neighbor as yourself." That's true! That's what it says! It also says "You shall love your straight neighbor as yourself." And the Word of God is clear that we are to show "no partiality."

> Colossians 3:12-14 (NRSV)
>
> As God's chosen ones, holy and beloved, clothe yourselves with compassion, kindness, humility, meekness, and patience. **Bear with one another** and, if anyone has a complaint against another, forgive each other; just as the Lord has forgiven you, so you also must forgive. Above all, clothe yourselves with love, which binds everything together in perfect harmony.

We must bear with one another. We must bear with each other's gayness and straightness.

> Romans 13:9-10 (NRSV)
>
> The Commandments, "You shall not commit adultery; you shall not murder; you shall not steal; you shall not covet;" and

any other commandment, are summed up in this word, "Love your neighbor as yourself." **Love does no wrong to a neighbor; therefore, love is the fulfilling of the law**.

The only law that God enforces is the Law of Love. It is not possible for any Christian to not love and not embrace and not support his or her gay fellow humans. All children are of God, made by God, and loved by God.

1 John 3:10-16 (NRSV)

The children of God and the children of the devil are revealed in this way: all who do not do what is right is not from God, nor are those who do not love their brothers and sisters. For this is the message you have heard from the beginning, that we should love one another. We must not be like Cain who was from the evil one and murdered his brother. And why did he murder him? Because his own deeds were evil and his brother's righteous. Do not be astonished, brothers and sisters, that the world hates you. We know that we have passed from death to life because we love one another. **Whoever does not love abides in death. All who hate a brother or sister are murderers**, and you know that murderers do not have eternal life abiding in them. We know that he laid down his life for us – and we ought to lay down our lives for one another.

If any man or woman or preacher or politician perpetuates anti-gay behaviors or laws, they are like murderers in the eyes of God. What would Jesus do? Would Jesus lay down his life for a gay man, woman, or child? I can answer that! He already did!

Hebrews 13:8 (NRSV)

Jesus Christ is the same yesterday, and today, and forever.

Judging Others - Proof 5

Only God can judge. We cannot.

I believe everyone at one time or another has sat through a church service that was inspiring and wonderful and true and uplifting only to have the pastor then throw in some comment about homosexuality and how *choosing* the *gay lifestyle* is against God and against his Word.

It can pretty much ruin your Sunday. And it is 100% a lie. First off, no one chooses his or her sexuality. If so, you should be able to tell me when you *chose* which way you were going to go. We have all experienced the fact that our sexuality chooses us.

But apart from that obvious lie, what is more surprising is that these speakers from the pulpits can rain down judgment on our homosexual brothers and sisters when the Bible is bursting with a very clear message that bars pastors (and others) from judging anyone. The clear message that is repeated over and over again throughout the Bible is *God alone is the judge of us.*

Psalm 75:2-7 (ESV)

At the set time that I appoint I will judge with equity. When the earth totters, with all its inhabitants, it is I who keep its pillars steady. Selah. I say to the boastful, "Do not boast," and to the wicked, "Do not lift up your horn; do not lift up your horn on high, or speak with insolent neck." For not from the east or from the west and not from the wilderness comes lifting up; **but it is God who executes judgment**, putting down one thing and lifting up another.

This means that every minister, every pastor, every priest, every denomination that has put homophobic rhetoric in their church doctrine, has placed themselves squarely against the Word of God in the Bible.

Are we to judge others? Let's study the Bible and see.

Using the most popular translation, the King James Version, in the Bible there are 670 verses that uses the word **judge** or derivative words such as **judged, judges, judgest, judgeth, judging, judgment,** or **judgments.**

In the Bible — which is a compilation of many writings over many time periods by different authors in different cultures — the word **judge** and its derivative words is frequently used but its meaning is different in different contexts.

In Biblical times, people used the word **judge** as a noun in the same way we use the word **judge** today, as a job title. Judges were (and are) people who uphold the law, make decisions between people who have legal issues between them, and, in Biblical times, judges took the part of a king or a policeman or a jury in these legal decisions between persons.

Also in the Bible the word **judge** is a verb and was often used in place of the word *decision*. If you were to make a decision whether to take the left fork in the road or the right fork, you would be *judging* which fork to take. This use of the word **judge** and its derivative words are just referring to a common decision, not a holy indictment.

If we go through the 670 verses and identify those verses where the word **judge** is a job title or the acts of a **Judge** (a good Judge or a bad Judge) or where the word is referring to a legal judgment in a civil action, or the word is referring to just making a personal decision, then we would find 252 verses that use the word **judge** in a manner that does not refer to a heavenly decree.

That leaves us with 418 other scriptures that use the word **judge** and its derivatives that does refer to a heavenly decree. These are:

Genesis 15:14, Genesis 16:5, Genesis 18:19, Genesis 18:25, Genesis 30:6, Genesis 31:53, Exodus 5:21, Exodus 6:6, Exodus 7:4, Exodus 12:12, Exodus 21:1, Exodus 24:3, Leviticus 18:4, Leviticus 18:5, Leviticus 18:26, Leviticus 19:37, Leviticus 20:22, Leviticus 25:18, Leviticus 26:15, Leviticus 26:43, Leviticus 26:46, Numbers 33:4, Numbers 36:13, Deuteronomy 1:17, Deuteronomy 4:1, Deuteronomy 4:5, Deuteronomy 6:20, Deuteronomy 8:11, Deuteronomy 11:1, Deuteronomy 11:32, Deuteronomy 12:1, Deuteronomy 26:16, Deuteronomy 26:17, Deuteronomy 30:16, Deuteronomy 32:4, Deuteronomy 32:36, Judges 11:27, 1 Samuel 2:10, 1 Samuel 2:25, 1 Samuel 3:13, 1 Samuel 24:12, 1 Samuel 24:15, 2 Samuel 22:23, 1 Kings 2:3, 1 Kings 6:12, 1 Kings 8:58, 1 Kings 9:4, 1 Kings 11:33, 1 Chronicles 16:12, 1 Chronicles 16:14, 1 Chronicles 16:33, 1 Chronicles 22:13, 1 Chronicles 28:7, 2 Chronicles 7:17, 2 Chronicles 19:8, 2 Chronicles 20:12, Ezra 7:10, Nehemiah 1:7, Nehemiah 9:13, Nehemiah 9:29, Nehemiah 10:29, Job 8:3, Job 9:15, Job 9:19, Job 9:32, Job 19:7, Job 19:29, Job 21:22, Job 22:4, Job 22:13, Job 23:7, Job 27:2, Job 29:14, Job 34:5, Job 34:12, Job 35:14, Job 36:17, Job 36:31, Job 37:23, Job 40:8, Psalms 1:5, Psalms 7:6, Psalms 7:8, Psalms 7:11, Psalms 9:4, Psalms 9:7, Psalms 9:8, Psalms 9:16, Psalms 9:19, Psalms 10:5, Psalms 10:18, Psalms 18:22, Psalms 19:9, Psalms 25:9, Psalms 26:1, Psalms 33:5, Psalms 35:23, Psalms 35:24, Psalms 36:6, Psalms 37:6, Psalms 37:28, Psalms 37:30, Psalms 43:1, Psalms 48:11, Psalms 50:4, Psalms 50:6, Psalms 51:4, Psalms 54:1, Psalms 58:11, Psalms 67:4, Psalms 68:5, Psalms 72:1, Psalms 72:2, Psalms 72:4, Psalms 75:7, Psalms 76:8, Psalms 76:9, Psalms 82:1, Psalms 82:2, Psalms 82:8, Psalms 89:14, Psalms 89:30, Psalms 94:2, Psalms 94:15, Psalms 96:10, Psalms 96:13, Psalms 97:2, Psalms 97:8, Psalms 98:9, Psalms 101:1, Psalms 103:6, Psalms 105:5, Psalms 105:7, Psalms 106:3, Psalms 110:6, Psalms 111:7, Psalms 119:7, Psalms 119:13, Psalms 119:20, Psalms 119:30, Psalms 119:39, Psalms 119:43, Psalms 119:52, Psalms 119:62, Psalms 119:66, Psalms 119:75, Psalms 119:84, Psalms 119:102, Psalms 119:106, Psalms 119:108, Psalms 119:120, Psalms 119:121, Psalms 119:137, Psalms 119:149, Psalms 119:156, Psalms 119:160, Psalms 119:164, Psalms 119:175, Psalms 122:5, Psalms 135:14, Psalms 143:2, Psalms 146:7, Psalms 147:19, Psalms 147:20, Psalms 149:9, Proverbs 1:3, Proverbs 2:8, Proverbs 2:9, Proverbs 8:20, Proverbs 13:23,

Proverbs 21:15, Proverbs 28:5, Proverbs 29:26, Proverbs 31:5, Ecclesiastes 3:16, Ecclesiastes 3:17, Ecclesiastes 8:5, Ecclesiastes 8:6, Ecclesiastes 11:9, Ecclesiastes 12:14, Isaiah 1:17, Isaiah 1:21, Isaiah 1:23, Isaiah 1:27, Isaiah 2:4, Isaiah 3:13, Isaiah 3:14, Isaiah 4:4, Isaiah 5:7, Isaiah 5:16, Isaiah 9:7, Isaiah 11:3, Isaiah 11:4, Isaiah 16:3, Isaiah 26:8, Isaiah 26:9, Isaiah 28:17, Isaiah 30:18, Isaiah 32:16, Isaiah 33:5, Isaiah 33:22, Isaiah 34:5, Isaiah 40:14, Isaiah 40:27, Isaiah 42:1, Isaiah 42:3, Isaiah 42:4, Isaiah 49:4, Isaiah 51:4, Isaiah 51:5, Isaiah 53:8, Isaiah 54:17, Isaiah 56:1, Isaiah 59:8, Isaiah 59:9, Isaiah 59:11, Isaiah 59:14, Isaiah 59:15, Isaiah 61:8, Jeremiah 1:16, Jeremiah 4:2, Jeremiah 5:1, Jeremiah 5:4, Jeremiah 5:5, Jeremiah 5:28, Jeremiah 7:5, Jeremiah 8:7, Jeremiah 9:24, Jeremiah 10:24, Jeremiah 11:20, Jeremiah 12:1, Jeremiah 21:12, Jeremiah 22:3, Jeremiah 22:15, Jeremiah 23:5, Jeremiah 33:15, Jeremiah 48:47, Jeremiah 49:12, Jeremiah 51:9, Jeremiah 51:47, Jeremiah 51:52, Lamentations 3:59, Ezekiel 5:6, Ezekiel 5:7, Ezekiel 5:8, Ezekiel 5:10, Ezekiel 5:15, Ezekiel 7:3, Ezekiel 7:8, Ezekiel 7:27, Ezekiel 11:9, Ezekiel 11:10, Ezekiel 11:11, Ezekiel 11:12, Ezekiel 14:21, Ezekiel 16:38, Ezekiel 16:52, Ezekiel 18:8, Ezekiel 18:9, Ezekiel 18:17, Ezekiel 18:30, Ezekiel 20:11, Ezekiel 20:13, Ezekiel 20:16, Ezekiel 20:18, Ezekiel 20:19, Ezekiel 20:21, Ezekiel 20:24, Ezekiel 20:25, Ezekiel 21:30, Ezekiel 23:24, Ezekiel 24:14, Ezekiel 25:11, Ezekiel 28:22, Ezekiel 28:23, Ezekiel 28:26, Ezekiel 30:14, Ezekiel 30:19, 3:20, Ezekiel 4:16, Ezekiel 34:17, Ezekiel 34:20, Ezekiel 34:22, Ezekiel 35:11, Ezekiel 36:19, Ezekiel 36:27, Ezekiel 37:24, Ezekiel 39:21, Ezekiel 44:24, Daniel 7:10, Daniel 7:22, Daniel 7:26, Daniel 9:5, Hosea 2:19, Hosea 5:1, Hosea 5:11, Hosea 6:5, Hosea 12:6, Joel 3:12, Amos 5:15, Amos 5:24, Micah 3:1, Micah 3:9, Micah 4:3, Micah 7:9, Habakkuk 1:12, Zephaniah 2:3, Zephaniah 3:5, Malachi 2:17, Malachi 3:5, Malachi 4:4, Matthew 5:21, Matthew 5:22, Matthew 7:1, Matthew 7:2, Matthew 10:15, Matthew 11:22, Matthew 11:24, Matthew 12:20, Matthew 12:36, Matthew 12:41, Matthew 12:42, Matthew 23:23, Mark 6:11, Luke 6:37, Luke 10:14, Luke 11:31, Luke 11:32, Luke 11:42, John 5:22, John 5:27, John 5:30, John 7:24, John 8:15, John 8:16, John 8:26, John 8:50, John 9:39, John 12:31, John 12:47, John 12:48, John 16:8, John 16:11, Acts 7:7, Acts 17:31, Acts 24:25, Romans 1:32, Romans 2:1, Romans 2:2, Romans 2:3, Romans 2:5, Romans 2:12, Romans 2:16, Romans 2:27, Romans 3:4, Romans 3:6, Romans 3:7, Romans 5:16, Romans 5:18, Romans 11:33, Romans 14:3, Romans 14:4, Romans 14:10, Romans 14:13, 1 Corinthians 1:10, 1 Corinthians 2:15, 1 Corinthians 4:3, 1 Corinthians 4:4, 1 Corinthians 4:5, 1 Corinthians 5:12, 1 Corinthians 5:13, 1 Corinthians 10:29, 1 Corinthians 11:31, 1 Corinthians 11:32, Galatians 5:10, Philippians 1:9, Colossians 2:16, 2 Thessalonians 1:5, 1 Timothy 5:24, 2 Timothy 4:1, 2 Timothy 4:8, Hebrews 6:2, Hebrews 9:27, Hebrews 10:27, Hebrews 10:30,

Hebrews 12:23, Hebrews 13:4, James 2:4, James 2:12, James 2:13, James 4:11, James 4:12, James 5:9, 1 Peter 1:17, 1 Peter 2:23, 1 Peter 4:5, 1 Peter 4:6, 1 Peter 4:17, 2 Peter 2:4, 2 Peter 2:9, 2 Peter 3:7, 1 John 4:17, Jude 1:6, Jude 1:15, Revelation 6:10, Revelation 11:18, Revelation 14:7, Revelation 15:4, Revelation 16:5, Revelation 16:7, Revelation 17:1, Revelation 18:8, Revelation 18:10, Revelation 19:2, Revelation 19:11, Revelation 20:4, Revelation 20:12, and Revelation 20:13

Now we can put these 418 verses into two categories.

The first and largest category — 390 verses — are all verses that use the word **judge** or any derivatives of the word **judge** that refer to God judging or to the judgment of God, or refers to the decisions of God, or refers to a decision based on the Word of God, or is referring to the judgment of God.

After seeing how many times the Word refers to God being the Judge, or God being the author of judgment, or God judging, it is clear that the Bible says **God is our Judge** and judges us. That is 390 instances out of 418 — about 93%.

The second category of verses in this group of 418 scriptures that use the word **judge** or derivatives of the word **judge** is a group of 28 verses that state **we are not to judge**. Here they are in order of appearance:

1) Isaiah 54:17 (KJV)

No weapon that is formed against thee shall prosper; and every tongue that shall rise against thee in judgment thou shalt condemn. This is the heritage of the servants of the LORD, and their righteousness is of me, saith the LORD.

No one is permitted to judge those who love God and who are serving God.

2) Ezekiel 16:52 (KJV)

Thou also, which hast judged thy sisters, bear thine own shame for thy sins that thou hast committed more abominable than they: they are more righteous than thou: yea, be thou confounded also, and bear thy shame, in that thou hast justified thy sisters.

A theme throughout the Bible is the teaching that one cannot judge another since one's own sins are just as bad or worse than the accused's sins.

> **3&4)** Matthew 5:21-22 (**Jesus quote**) (NRSV)
>
> You have heard that it was said to those of ancient times, "You shall not murder"; and "Whoever murders shall be liable to judgment." But I say to you that if you are angry with a brother or sister, you will be liable to judgment; and if you insult a brother or sister, you will be liable to the counsel; and if you say, "You fool," you will be liable to the hell of fire.

Insulting someone (judging their character) and expressing anger against someone (judging their behavior or motives) is likened to murder and, therefore, puts you in the wrong and qualifies you to be judged by God.

> **5)** Matthew 7:1 (**Jesus quote**) (KJV)
>
> Judge not, that ye be not judged.

> **6)** Matthew 7:2 (**Jesus quote**) (KJV)
>
> For with what judgment ye judge, ye shall be judged: and with what measure ye mete, it shall be measured to you again.

I'm Rubber. You're Glue. Whatever you say bounces off me and sticks on you. (So don't.)

> **7)** Luke 6:37 (**Jesus quote**) (KJV)
>
> Judge not, and ye shall not be judged: condemn not, and ye shall not be condemned: forgive, and ye shall be forgiven:

> **8)** John 8:15, (**Jesus quote**) (KJV)
>
> Ye judge after the flesh; I judge no man.

> **9)** John 12:47 (**Jesus quote**) (KJV)
>
> And if any man hear my words, and believe not, I judge him not: for I came not to judge the world, but to save the world.

Jesus is not the condemner. He does not even condemn those who do not believe in him. And we are to be like Jesus. In these words of Jesus in the scripture above, it is clear that we are not to judge others. When he was asked whether the crowd should condemn the woman caught in adultery, (John 8:7) Jesus just drew in the dirt with a stick until he heard from his Father God what to say (John 5:19). Only then did he speak and say, "He who is without sin, cast the first stone."

Jesus was always confronting the vindictive and punitive culture of his time and people's view of God as a punishing God. Because of him, we better understand the Bible and know that God is our only Judge and God himself has blotted out our sins forever (Isaiah 43:25).

> **10)** Romans 2:1 (KJV)
>
> Therefore thou art inexcusable, O man, whosoever thou art that judgest: for wherein thou judgest another, thou condemnest thyself; for thou that judgest doest the same things.

> **11)** Romans 2:3 (KJV)
>
> And thinkest thou this, O man, that judgest them which do such things, and doest the same, that thou shalt escape the judgment of God?

Anyone who is claiming to be a Christian and is judging gays (or anyone else for that matter) and speaking as if they themselves have the authority of Heaven to judge their gay brothers and sisters, is not reading (or believing) their Bible.

Paul had the same problem in the early Church with his congregation judging the new Gentile converts. The early Church was originally all Jews and so they were keeping all the Jewish customs and also, at the same time, proclaiming the message and victory of Jesus the Christ.

The Jews had taken the Ten Commandments that God gave them (and that Jesus later boiled down to two commandments in Matthew 22:37 - 40) and turned them into 613 laws covering everything from the correct manner of ritual sacrifice to the correct timing for sex, what to wear, what to eat, and how to dispose of human waste. We know that these new laws, all these many rules for everything in life, were not from God because Jesus said Moses permitted divorce (Deuteronomy 24:1) because the *people* insisted, and that God hates divorce (Malachi 2:16). And *that* divorce law was supposedly from God. So just having the law come from Moses does not guarantee it is from God.

In the early Church, when Gentiles (anyone not Jewish) joined the Christian Church, it was a problem for the Jews. The question was 'Could you be a good Christian and not also follow all the laws Moses handed down?' 'Is it OK to mingle with these Gentiles?' 'Don't these new non-Jewish believers need to get circumcised?' 'Don't they need to keep kosher?'

God told Peter specifically that it was OK to speak to Gentile believers (Acts 10:28 - 29). And Paul had to re-preach the entire gospel of Christ to the church so they can apply the teachings of Christ to these issues. This is at the center of Christian teaching, that we are all now Christ's and are blameless, sinless, and answerable only to God. We are no longer bound by the law. These 613 traditional laws of the Jewish custom are neutral. Don't judge anyone who follows these laws and don't judge anyone who does not keep these laws. We are all free.

12) Romans 2:27 (KJV)

And shall not uncircumcision which is by nature, if it fulfill the law, judge thee, who by the letter and circumcision dost transgress the law?

13) Romans 14:3 (KJV)

Let not him that eateth despise him that eateth not; and let not him which eateth not judge him that eateth: for God hath received him.

14) Romans 14:4 (KJV)

Who art thou that judgest another man's servant? to his own master he standeth or falleth. Yea, he shall be holden up: for God is able to make him stand.

15) Romans 14:10 (KJV)

But why dost thou judge thy brother? or why dost thou set at naught thy brother? for we shall all stand before the judgment seat of Christ.

16) Romans 14:13 (KJV)

Let us not therefore judge one another any more: but judge (decide) this rather, that no man put a **stumblingblock** or an occasion to fall in his brother's way.

Any preacher or any Christian who opens their mouth and suggests to any gay person that they are not the apple of God's eye and are not 100% loved just as they are now has put a 'stumblingblock' before that person through their negative judgment.

17) 1 Corinthians 2:15 (KJV)

But he that is spiritual judgeth all things (for himself), yet he himself is judged of no man.

Our God-given Sprit, the Spirit of Christ, is our true guide inside of us and will always point the way for us to go, but no human being can judge us.

18) 1 Corinthians 4:3 (KJV)

But with me it is a very small thing that I should be judged of you, or of man's judgment: yea, I judge not mine own self.

Paul is saying, "I do not care that anyone judges me. I do not even judge myself."

19) 1 Corinthians 4:4 (KJV)

For I know nothing by myself; yet am I not hereby justified: but he that judgeth me is the Lord.

20) 1 Corinthians 4:5 (KJV)

Therefore judge nothing before the time, until the Lord come, who both will bring to light the hidden things of darkness, and will make manifest the counsels of the hearts: and then shall every man have praise of God.

21) 1 Corinthians 5:12 (KJV)

For what have I to do to judge them also that are without? **do not ye judge them that are within**?

Let's pause here.

The verse immediately above is a fragment from the letter to the church in Corinth from Paul addressing a lot of problems in that church that some people have now used to claim that the Bible says we *are* to judge others, seeming to say that we are to judge those within our own ranks.

This area of Paul's letter uses the word **judge** and derivative words in many meanings all within a few words of each other—God's spiritual judgment, judging to form an opinion of a person that is negative, and judging a legal issue between two parties. Here is the larger passage, to provide context, and followed by my comments.

NOTE: In the King James translation of the Bible, words in italics are words that are not in the Bible but that were added at the discretion of the translator. For clarity, I will delete the words the King James Version has in italics in this passage.

1 Corinthians 5:12 in context: **1 Corinthians 5:9 through 6:8** (KJ21)

I wrote unto you in an epistle not to company with fornicators; Yet not altogether with the fornicators of this world, or with the covetous, or extortioners, or with idolators; for then must ye needs go out of the world.

(I said not to buddy up with sinners but I didn't mean to never to be with sinners for then you would not be able to live on planet Earth.)

But I now have written unto you not to keep company, if any man that is called a brother be a fornicator, or covetous, or an idolater, or a railer, or a drunkard, or an extortioner; with such an one no not to eat.

(But now I say it again, steer clear of those so-called Christians, those who call themselves Christian but who are not behaving like a Christian.)

For what have I to do to judge them also that are without?

(I do not bother to judge anyone but especially those who are outside the Church.)

Do not ye judge them that are within?

(I have told you not to judge each other but I know you are still at it.)

But them that are without God judgeth.

(But these false Christians are of the world, so just ignore them and let God judge them.)

Therefore put away from among yourselves that wicked person.

(Steer clear of these trouble-makers. They are making problems in the Church.)

Dare any of you, having a matter against another, go to law before the unjust, and not before the saints?

(Am I understanding correctly that some of you are taking each other to court and airing your problems with each other in public?)

Do ye not know that the saints shall judge the world?

(You will be qualified to judge such things in Heaven)?

And if the world shall be judged by you, are ye unworthy to judge the smallest matters?

(You can handle these petty grievances on your own because God has given you authority in Heaven so he certainly has given you enough authority on Earth to decide these legal issues between yourselves.)

Know ye not that we shall judge angels? How much more things that pertain to this life? If then ye have judgments of things pertaining to this life, set them to judge who are least esteemed in the church.

(These issues between your church members are so simple that you can get the least educated among you to decide these matters.)

I speak to your shame. Is it so, that there is not a wise man among you? No, not one that shall be able to judge between his brethren? But brother goeth to law with brother, and that before the unbelievers.

(This is embarrassing that your church members are suing each other in open court.)

Now therefore there is utterly a fault among you, because ye go to law with one another. Why do ye not rather take wrong? Why do ye not rather be defrauded? Nay, ye do wrong, and defraud, and that brethren.

(If you guys can't settle these squabbles in-house, then it is better that you don't settle them at all, don't even go to court, just let it go. Turn the other cheek. You're not so perfect.)

In this letter to the Church, Paul does not say we can stand in judgment of our fellow man. Indeed, he restates the truth. We are not to judge each other.

22) 1 Corinthians 10:29 (KJV)

Conscience, I say, not thine own, but of the other: for why is my liberty judged of another man's conscience?

We are in liberty in Jesus. We are free to be ourselves in Christ. Ignore other's opinions.

23) 1 Corinthians 11:31 (KJV)

For if we would judge ourselves, we should not be judged.

We know we are not perfect. This is why we judge ourselves and it is important for us to know we are not perfect. For if we remain humble in this knowledge, that we are all sinners, God does not negatively judge us (because we have already judged ourselves).

24) Colossians 2:16 (KJV)

Let no man therefore judge you in meat, or in drink, or in respect of an holyday, or of the new moon, or of the sabbath days:

Some people have an idea of what is a true Christian, how a true Christian behaves, what lifestyle a true Christian lives. And they would be wrong.

25) James 2:3-5 (ASV) (two verses added here to give context to the single reference 'judges')

...and ye have regard to him that weareth the fine clothing, and say, Sit thou here in a good place; and ye say to the poor man, Stand thou there, or sit under my footstool; Do ye not make distinctions among yourselves, and become judges with evil thoughts? Hearken, my beloved brethren; did not God choose them that are poor as to the world to be rich in faith, and heirs of the kingdom which he promised to them that love him?

Any thought in your head that a person is worthy based on the fact that they appear to be rich or the idea that another person is unworthy based on the fact that they appear to be poor is an evil thought and you have become an evil judge of this world by your own thoughts. You cannot judge the quality of a person by any external attribute.

26) James 4:11 (KJV)

Speak not evil one of another, brethren. He that speaketh evil of his brother, and judgeth his brother, speaketh evil of the law, and judgeth the law: but if thou judge the law, thou art not a doer of the law, but a judge.

What is the law? To love God with all our heart and to love one another. If you are judging others, you are outside the law.

> **27)** James 4:12 (KJV)
>
> There is one lawgiver, who is able to save and to destroy: who art thou that judgest another?

> **28)** James 5:9 (KJV)
>
> Grudge not one against another, brethren, lest ye be condemned: behold, the judge standeth before the door.

There is only one God and you are not he, so you can't judge anyone.

So how many verses in the Bible say _we_ are the Judge of our fellow man? Zero. The facts are tabulated, and the score looks like the chart on the next page.

Gay—the last Church bigotry.

Depending on how old you are and maybe also depending on where you were raised, when you hear the word _bigot_ your mind goes to a particular bigotry. Racism? Anti-Semitism? Sexism? These are large bigot categories.

The established church has struggled against gender issues and race issues and anti-Semitism for centuries. And progress is being made. But now Christian church leaders focus more on our faith's Jewish roots, and it is rare for churches to insist women shouldn't be pastors. Congregations continue to become more racially blended as our communities become more racially blended.

But the gay issue remains a sticking point for many churches and denominations. This is just bigotry, not God.

Does the white person believe himself to be superior to a black person?

Does the black person believe himself to be superior to a white person?

Does the man feel himself to be superior to a woman?

Does the woman feel herself to be superior to a man?

Does the straight person believe himself to be superior to the gay person?

Does the gay person believe himself to be superior to the straight person?

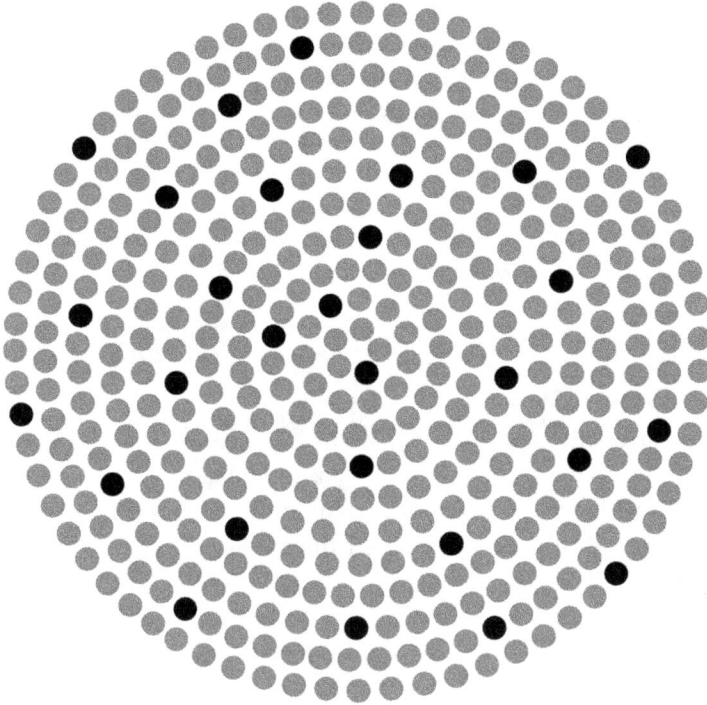

Judging

● Represents the 390 scriptures that say God is judge, God judges, or refers to judgement of God.

● Represents the 28 scriptures that say we aree not to judge others.

▨ Represents scriptures that say we are the judge (oops - none here, sorry)

1 Corinthians 4:7 (NLT)

For what gives you the right to make such a judgment? What do you have that God hasn't given you? **And if everything you have is from God, why boast as though it were not a gift?**

It is to no one's credit that they were born white or black or male or female or gay or straight. These are not accomplishments. Were you born a black female lesbian? It's a gift from God. Were you born a white straight Jew? It's a gift from God. The verse above is Paul reminding us that everything we have comes as a gift so we cannot boast about ourselves, as if we are something special since we didn't do anything, but merely received a free gift. And it is the same for every feature of us. God made us all just the way we are.

John 1:3 (AKJV)

All things were made by him; and without him was not any thing made that was made.

We are full of gifts from God.

So what we have and what we are is a gift from God—our gender, our sexual orientation, our race, our eye color, our nationality, our talents — all of it. The only issue in our life is: What are we going to do with the gifts God has given us? We can never think ourselves better than anyone else because of these free gifts that we did not earn.

Do not assume you know who is going to Heaven and who is going to Hell. You can only know about yourself.

Romans 10:9-13 (NRSV)

Because if you confess with your lips that Jesus is Lord and believe in your heart that God raised him from the dead, you will be saved. For one believes with the heart and so is justified, and one confesses with the mouth and so is saved. The Scripture says "No one who believes in him will be put to shame." **For there is no distinction between Jew and Greek; the same Lord is Lord of all and is generous to all who call upon him.** For, "Everyone who calls on the name of the Lord shall be saved."

So if we can't have opinions about other people, how do we behave?

If you look at the tone adopted by many of the Church authorities and spokespersons for Jesus, it seems that they are crowing like roosters on a barn roof about their superiority. But Jesus said the meek shall inherit the Earth. And he exhorts us to be humble and gentle with each other and to give no offense to any man.

The following is a story that Jesus tells. Jesus knows he's speaking to a group that think that they are religiously superior and that everyone else is inferior to them.

> Luke 18:9-14 (KJV)
>
> And he spake this parable unto certain which trusted in themselves that they were righteous, and despised others: "Two men went up to the temple to pray, one a Pharisee and the other a tax collector. The Pharisee stood and prayed thus with himself, "**God, I thank you that I am not like other men** – extortioners, unjust, adulterers, or even as this tax collector. I fast twice a week; I give tithes of all that I possess." And the tax collector, standing afar off, would not so much as raise his eyes to heaven, but beat his breast, saying, "God, be merciful to me a sinner!" I tell you, this man went down to his house justified rather than the other; for everyone who exalts himself will be humbled, and he who humbles himself will be exalted."

In those days the sanctimonious, holier-than-thou types, would stand on street corners and pray loudly to show how spiritual they were. In this story Jesus tells, it seems probable that the tax collector can hear the loud prayer of the Pharisee. The Pharisee may even believe his loud prayers will serve as religious instruction for the unholy tax collector. The story only falls short of becoming a comedy routine when the tax collector doesn't respond in kind and so doesn't include the Pharisee in his prayers.

I understand that there's a classic prayer that says "Thank you, God, that you did not make me a woman." I am sure it would be hilarious to have a man calling loudly to God saying "Thank you, God, for not making me a woman" and right next to him is his wife praying loudly to God "Dear God, thank you for not making me a man."

We should all be grateful for the free gifts we have received from God. All things we are given and did not give ourselves are gifts. And we do not have the authority to judge anyone else's gifts.

Be humble, forgive one another, and give no offense.

What a blessing it would be to attend a church where people were not critical of anyone but, rather, were humble, forgave one another, and refused to give any offense to anyone. That would be such a stark contrast to the culture we see mirrored to us in the world.

> Matthew 6:14-15 (NRSV)
>
> **For if you forgive others their trespasses, your heavenly Father will also forgive you**; but if you do not forgive others, neither will your Father forgive your trespasses.

Not one of us has the authority to forgive ourselves, so we can only forgive each other and then God forgives us. It is a perfect system.

> Romans 15:1-3 (NRSV)
>
> We who are strong ought to put up with the failings of the weak, and not to please ourselves. Each of us must please our neighbor for the good purpose of building up the neighbor. **For Christ did not please himself; but, it is written, "The insults of those who insult you have fallen on me."**

If you insult homosexuals, you are insulting God who made them and who loves them.

1 Corinthians 10:30-11:1 (NKJV)

But if I partake with thanks, why am I evil spoken of for the food over which I give thanks? Therefore, whether you eat or drink, or what ever you do, do all to the glory of God. **Give no offense, either to the Jews or to the Greeks or to the church of God, just as I also please all men in all things, not seeking my own profit, but the profit of many, that they may be saved**. Imitate me, just as I also imitate Christ.

Be ye doers of the Word.

Sadly, Christians are famous for saying one thing and doing another. But we are blessed in that we have God's Word in the Holy Bible. If we want to truly know how God thinks of us — what God wants us to do, how God made us, how God wants us to treat each other — we have only to read his Word and then do it.

James 1:22 (KJV)

But be ye doers of the Word and not hearers only, deceiving your own selves.

Sexual Sin - Proof 6

Terms that refer to sexual sin must be defined scripturally or else we miss God's message.

There are several terms that are used in certain translations of the Bible that are improperly used today to claim that the Bible is referring to homosexuality—terms such as *sexual immorality*, *sexual sin*, *sodomy*, and *unnatural*. But none of these terms in the Bible are referring to gay people or gay sex. And I will prove it.

First, what is *sexual sin* or *sexual immorality*?

Ask anyone what exactly is Biblical *sexual immorality* or *sexual sin* and the answers will be either what they themselves believe to be sexually immoral or what they believe the Bible would say is sexually immoral.

The two terms are unhelpfully vague and yet these two terms appear many times in contemporary Bible translations, almost inviting the reader to replace these phrases with their own ideas of what is Biblical sexual misconduct, leading certain Christian ministers to imply that these two terms refer to homosexuality.

The King James translation of the Bible of 1611—the basis for many later Biblical translations—does not use the terms *sexual immorality* or *sexual sin*.

To understand what these other, later translators call *sexual immorality* or *sexual sin,* we have to conduct a parallel study of terms. This study reveals that, in every case, the translators' use of the term *sexual immorality* and *sexual sin* in other, later, translations was originally the word *fornication* in the King James Version.

> **Parallel Study:** All the verses below use the word *fornication* or *fornicator(s)* in the King James Version where that same word is later replaced with *sexual sin* or *sexual immorality* in certain other translations: Ezekiel 16:26, Matthew 5:32, Matthew 15:19, Matthew19:9, Mark 7:21, John 8:41, Acts 15:20, Acts 15:29, Acts 21:25, Romans 1:29, 1 Corinthians 5:1, 1 Corinthians 5:9, 1 Corinthians 5:10, 1 Corinthians 5:11, 1 Corinthians 6:9, 1 Corinthians 6:13, 1 Corinthians 6:18, 1 Corinthians 7:2, 1 Corinthians 10:8, 2 Corinthians 12:21, Galatians 5:19, Ephesians 5:3, Colossians 3:5, 1 Thessalonians 4:3, Hebrews 12:16, Jude 1:6-7, Revelation 2:14, Revelation 2:20, Revelation 2:21, Revelation 9:21, Revelation 14:8, Revelation 17:2, Revelation 17:4, Revelation 18:3, Revelation 18:9, and Revelation 19:2.

In the original King James translation there are an additional four verses that also use the word *fornication* but that are not translated as *sexual immorality* or *sexual sin* in later translations: 2 Chronicles 21:11, Isaiah 23:17, Ezekiel 16:15 and Ezekiel 16:29. In these four verses, the word *fornication* is later translated as *whore* or *prostitute.* But no one can say that *whore* or *prostitute* means *gay.*

If all the other 36 verses in the King James Version that refer to *fornication* are translated elsewhere as *sexual immorality* or *sexual sin,* then what does *fornication* actually mean?

What is fornication?

The Bible is clear. *Sexual immorality* or *sexual sin*—fornication—is using or abusing others through sex: Sexual Exploitation.

For this is the will of God, your sanctification: that you abstain from **fornication**; that each one of you know how to control your own body in holiness and honor, not with lustful passion, like the Gentiles who do not know God; **that no one wrong or exploit a brother or sister in this matter,** because the Lord is an avenger in all these things, just as we have already told you beforehand and solemnly warned you. For God did not call us to impurity but in holiness. Therefore whoever rejects this rejects not human authority but God, who also gives his Holy Spirit to you.

Fornication is the exploitation of another human being, gay or straight, through sex. Any sexual relationship that is using another person for sex is not of God. That includes mindless one-night-stands, whoring and prostitution. That includes rape. Therefore, any sexual relationship that comes from a caring place—gay or straight—is of God. It is all about relationship.

Fornication (*sexual immorality* or *sexual sin*)—sex acts that are not part of a caring relationship, is the sin that hurts you as much as it hurts the other person.

The verse above is from Paul's letter to the church at Thessalonica in Greece. Paul wrote this in Greek to the Greeks. And it is apt as the ancient Greek culture of that time was one of rampant sexual exploitation by men who were raised in a world where it was routine and expected for men to sexually exploit both men and women as an exercise of one's social superiority and masculine dominance.

This is 1 Corinthians 6:18 in both the King James Version (KJV) and the English Standard Version (ESV), written by Paul to the Christians in Greece:

1 Corinthians 6:18 (KJV)

Flee fornication. Every sin that a man doeth is without the body: **but he that committeth fornication sinneth against his own body.**

1 Corinthians 6:18 (ESV)

Flee from sexual immorality. Every other sin a person commits is outside the body, **but the sexually immoral person sins against his own body**.

Sex for the sake of sex can lead to sex addiction or pornography addiction which will, over time, destroy the body's ability to sexually perform in a healthy and positive way. But culturally embedded sexual exploitation is even more powerful, supporting a world-view of domination and superiority over others, a world-view that is not compatible with the teachings of Jesus.

There is a commonly held belief that Biblical fornication is just another word for sex outside of marriage, such as pre-marital sex. But that would be inaccurate.

1 Corinthians 7:2 (KJV)

Nevertheless, to avoid **fornication**, let every man have his own wife, and let every woman have her own husband.

In the scripture above, it can seem that the Bible is saying "get married so you won't fornicate". But in the ancient Jewish world, in the Old Testament in Biblical times, having sex with someone you care about is how a man takes a wife or wives.

In the Jewish Biblical world, men were permitted multiple wives and legal sexual access to female slaves and workers (*concubines*) that included their wives' maids and staff. This is a very generous system from the male point-of-view, with a man permitted legal sexual relationships with almost all the women in his household. And the man in these relationships has also taken on responsibilities to those women that goes beyond sexual access.

The Bible has many verses warning the married man not to pursue sex outside his own multiple legal sexual relationships, especially not with a woman who is married to someone else, imploring him to, instead, go to professionals:

Proverbs 6:23-26 (NRSV)

For the commandment is a lamp and the teaching a light, and the reproofs of discipline are the way of life, to preserve you from the wife of another, from the smooth tongue of the **adulterous**. Do not desire her beauty in your heart, and do not let her capture you with her eyelashes; for **prostitute's** fee is only a loaf of bread, but the wife of another stalks a man's very life.

For the Jewish male adulterer, there were no additional obligations to a woman who is married to another man. Her husband has those responsibilities. So the Bible says it is wise for a man to pay for the services of a prostitute. The Old Testament says that sex with a prostitute results in only a fee. Presumably it is worth paying this fee rather than to start anything that will turn into a huge social problem.

The man who has sex with a married woman is committing fornication, taking the sex and forgoing the relational obligations. The man who has sex with a prostitute is also committing fornication, using her for sex without any further relational obligations.

However, according to the prophet Hosea, God promises to forgive the sin of fornication and adultery on the basis of fairness:

Hosea 4:14 (WEB, ASV, DBY, WBS, NASB, RSV, NIV)

I will not punish your daughters when they **play the prostitute**, nor **your brides when they commit adultery**; because the **men consort with prostitutes**, and **they sacrifice with the shrine prostitutes**; so the people without understanding will come to ruin.

So, yes, it is a sin, but it's complicated.

Prostitution

There is a prostitute in the Bible, Rehab, who saved the Hebrew Army and was responsible for Joshua's victory at Jericho. Later she married and became part of the lineage of Jesus. The prophet Hosea was instructed by God to marry a prostitute (who would prove to be unfaithful to him). And one young frustrated Jewish widow, Tamar, pretended to be a prostitute just so she could have sexual relations and (finally) become pregnant which was her legal right. One of her twin boys from this sexual union, Peretz, was later the great-grandfather of David, so she, Tamar, is also in the lineage of Jesus.

But in the scripture above, Hosea 4:14, the prophet describes the men of the day not only buying the services of conventional prostitutes but also of giving money to (and having sex with) shrine prostitutes which is idolatry—a sin against God by worshipping other gods before him.

Male and female temple prostitutes

There are many times where the Bible uses the word *prostitute* that refers to temple prostitutes. Deuteronomy 23:17 forbids Jewish women to be prostitutes though this is strictly a ban against cult prostitution, a practice within popular pagan sex religions.

Deuteronomy 23:17 (KJV)

There shall be **no whore of the daughters of Israel**, nor a **sodomite of the sons of Israel**.

I believe this verse is referring only to temple prostitutes as it links the word *whore* to the word *sodomite* which is the term for male temple prostitutes.

Hosea 4:17-18 (NRSV)

Ephraim is joined to idols – let him alone. When their drinking is ended, **they indulge in sexual orgies**; they love lewdness more than their glory.

1 Kings 14:24 (NRSV)

There were also male Temple prostitutes in the land. They committed all the abominations of the nations that the Lord drove out before the people of Israel.

1 Kings 15:11-12 (NRSV)

Asa did what was right in the sight of the Lord, as his father David had done. He put away the **male Temple prostitutes** of the land, and removed all the idols that his ancestors had made.

In the Old Testament, simple prostitution was a woman earning her living and supporting her children through the selling of her sexual favors to married men on a personal transaction basis. Temple prostitutes were in a totally different category involving group sex on the temple grounds where congregants experienced orgiastic sexual congress with both male and female cult prostitutes as part of their worship service. The contrast makes simple prostitution seem sweet and old-fashioned.

Old Testament and New Testament—it's a man's world.

The first book of the New Testament was written almost 500 years after the last part of the Old Testament was written (Malachi, the last book of the Neviim contained in the Tanakh). So there is a long period of time between the Hebrew Old Testament and the Greek New Testament.

However, there are similarities between the sexual world of ancient Jewish life of the Old Testament and the sexual world of ancient Greek life of the New Testament, but with an important difference.

In the Greek New Testament world, like the ancient Jewish Old Testament world, men were permitted legal sexual access to female slaves and female workers that included their wives' maids and staff. But, in addition to legal sexual relations with almost all the women in his household, the adult married Greek man was additionally expected to seduce a younger male with gifts, expose that young man to the finer things of life, and to also have sex with the young man.

The married man was then expected to dump the boy when he starts to grow facial hair. Then the married man was expected to go find a new young (male) sex object.

The discarded (and now older) young man was expected to join the military where he would engage in more male-on-male sex and then he was expected to marry some sheltered young woman when his military service was over. He would then start a family and then go to find *his* first young man to seduce.

These were not gay men. All these fellows were straight. They were just acting out the rite-of-passage ritual of their culture, sanctioned by the State and lauded as a superior way to tutor young males in the refinements of a life properly lived as a Greek citizen.

It is to this population that the New Testament is addressed. In the verses below from a letter to the church in Corinth, Greece, Paul lists the sorts of persons who "shall not inherit the Kingdom of God."

> 1 Corinthians 6:9-10 (KJV)
>
> Know ye not that the unrighteous shall not inherit the kingdom of God? Be not deceived: neither **fornicators**, nor **idolaters**, nor **adulterers**, nor **effeminate**, nor **abusers of themselves with mankind**, nor thieves, nor covetous, nor drunkards, nor revilers, nor extortioners, shall inherit the kingdom of God."

Adulterers and **fornicators** are both listed here so these terms are not interchangeable and the words do not mean *gay*. **Idolaters** in the New Testament refers to the practitioners of the many pagan religions of the time (every Greek god had their own following).

The word translated as **effeminate** in this verse is the Greek word **malakos** which is the passive partner in the male-on-male sex act, either a young boy or a temple prostitute, depending upon the translator. And **abusers of themselves with mankind** comes from the Greek word **arsenokoites**. This word has been controversial. It's not even in Strong's Greek Dictionary since it is not possible to know for sure what this word actually means. But there is growing support for this being Paul's word for the active partner in the male-on-male sex act.

These men were not gay. These were straight men schooled from puberty to routinely engage in male-on-male sex as an expression of one's social and masculine dominance over others.

Abusers of themselves with mankind

The term, **abusers of themselves with mankind,** seen in the verse above, is exclusive to the various King James translations (Authorized King James Version, New King James and the 21st Century King James). This term is translated from the Greek word, **arsenokoitai** which is only used twice in the Bible. Those two Biblical mentions are 1 Corinthians 6:9 (see above) and 1 Timothy 1:10 where **arsenokoitai** is translated here below as **defile themselves with mankind**:

> 1 Timothy 1:9-11 (KJV)
>
> [9] Knowing this, that the law is not made for a righteous man, but for the lawless and disobedient, for the ungodly and for sinners, for unholy and profane, for murderers of fathers and murderers of mothers, for manslayers, [10] For whoremongers, for them that **defile themselves with mankind**, for menstealers, for liars, for perjured persons, and if there be any other thing that is contrary to sound doctrine; [11] According to the glorious gospel of the blessed God, which was committed to my trust.

This King James wording in 1 Corinthians led many to assume this term referred to masturbation (hence the archaic euphemism, *self-abuse*) as masturbation was considered a terrible sexual sin by Thomas Aquinas, [Summa Theologica (1265-1274) II-II, q. 154, art. 12]. This Greek term **arsenokoital** has had people guessing for centuries.

But, in fact, these two New Testament verses repeat the same admonition that was given in the Old Testament in Leviticus 18:12 and Leviticus 20:13 in which straight men are forbidden to lie with straight men. So Paul is saying in Greek what the Old Testament said in Hebrew—that it was sin for a straight man to sexually penetrate a straight man.

It is notable that Paul did not at any time single out what today we would call lesbians for censure. And yet there were many first century Greek words for what we would today call lesbianism: *dihetaristriai, frictrix, hetairstrai, lesbiai, tribades,* or *tribas.*

And there were several first century Greek words for what we would today call gay men: *euryproktoi, kinaidos, arrenomanes,* or *pathikos.*

Thank you to Richard Brentlinger, former pastor and Biblical researcher, for his study of First Century Greek terms for gay and lesbian and related sexual terms. http://www. gaychristian101.com

Paul would not be at a loss for words to express himself on this issue if this is what he wished to communicate. But he did not. Paul does not anywhere in the New Testament mention as sins what we would today consider male gay sex nor female gay sex.

Sodomites

Where the Bible says **sodomite** (lower-case), it comes from the same term that is elsewhere used to denote a male shrine prostitute in both the Old Testament and New Testament.

> 1 Kings 15:12 (KJV)
>
> He put away the **sodomites** out of the land, and removed all the idols that his fathers had made.

In this verse the term *sodomites* is translated in many scriptural versions as *male shrine prostitutes* (New International Version 1984), as *male and female shrine prostitutes* (New Living Translation 2007), as *male cult prostitutes* (English Standard Version 2001 and New American Standard Bible 1995) and as *male prostitutes* (God's Word Translation 1995, and King James 2000 Bible, 2003).

> 2 Kings 23:7 (KJV)
>
> He broke down the houses of the **sodomites**, that were in the house of Yahweh, where the women wove hangings for the Asherah.

The Asherah was a pagan goddess, so this verse describes a place where people were using part of the temple that was meant for the worship of God, Yahweh, for the use of this pagan goddess, Asherah, hanging art around it to identify that that part of the temple was for this pagan worship.

Again, in this verse the term *sodomites* is translated as *male shrine prostitutes* (New International Version 1984), as *male and female shrine prostitutes* (New Living Translation 2007), as *male cult prostitutes* (English Standard Version 2001 and New American Standard Bible 1995) and as *male prostitutes* (God's Word Translation 1995, and King James 2000 Bible, 2003). So the Bible is not referring to gay people. It is referring to people commercially involved with this orgiastic, pornographic-style pagan idol worship.

Paul, in his letter to the church in Rome, did a good job of describing one of the pagan sex worship sessions as a Roman orgy:

> Romans 1:18-19, 21-27 (NRSV)
>
> For the wrath of God is revealed from heaven against all ungodliness and wickedness of those who by their wickedness suppress the truth. ... for though they knew God, they did not honor him as God or give thanks to him, but they became futile in their thinking, and their senseless minds were darkened. Claiming to be wise, they became fools; and they exchanged the glory of the immortal God for images resembling a mortal human being or birds or four-footed animals or reptiles. **Therefore God gave them up in the lusts of their hearts to impurity, to the degrading of their bodies among**

themselves, because they exchanged the truth about God for a lie and worshiped and served the creature (the idol) rather than the Creator, who is forever! Amen. For this reason, God gave them up to degrading passions. Their women exchanged natural intercourse for unnatural, and in the same way also the men, giving up natural intercourse with women, were consumed with passion for one another. Men committed shameless acts with men and received in their own persons the due penalty for their error.

The verses above—describing sex between men and sex between women and sex between men and women in an orgiastic environment—do not portray people in relationships. These are not people who are dating each other. These are not gay relationships. Rather, the Bible here is describing the popular pagan practices of the day that involved sexual orgies as an important part of their ritual worship. And because these practices involved idolatry, the Bible says it led to sexual behavior that was not natural to that person—solely because that person had strayed from worshiping God and so had committed something that is not of his or her own nature and it had overtaken him or her mentally. Today this can be described as something like contemporary pornography addiction, or sex addiction.

People that are sex addicts become involved in sex acts that are not, in fact, related to their sexual orientation. It is sex for the sake of sex with whoever and whatever. That fact—that people in the throes of extreme sex addictions do cross their own natural gender orientation boundaries—is well documented.

The person that continually engages in negative sexual activities will, over time, destroy their body's ability to perform in a healthy and positive way sexually. Martin Downs, who has a Master of Public Health degree from the Dartmouth Institute for Health Policy and Clinical Practice (TDI), wrote on the subject which was published on WebMD:

> In November 2004, a panel of experts testified before a Senate subcommittee that a product which millions of Americans

consume is dangerously addictive. They were talking about pornography.

The effects of porn on the brain were called "toxic" and compared to cocaine. One psychologist claimed, "prolonged exposure to pornography stimulates a preference for depictions of group sex, sadomasochistic practices, and sexual contact with animals."

Mary Anne Layden, PhD, a psychologist at the University of Pennsylvania, was one of the witnesses at the Senate hearing on pornography addiction. She says the same criteria used to diagnose problems like pathological gambling and substance abuse can be applied to problematic porn use.

One of the key features of addiction, she says, is the development of a tolerance to the addictive substance. In the way that drug addicts need increasingly larger doses to get high, she reports that porn addicts need to see more and more extreme material to feel the same level of excitement that they first experienced.

"Most of the addicts will say, well, here's the stuff I would never look at, it's so disgusting I would never look at it, whatever that is—sex with kids, sex with animals, sex involving feces," she says. "At some point they often cross over."

This is what God wants us to avoid — sexual contortion that has people acting out what is not in their own nature.

Sodom and Gomorrah

In some circles, the very names of the cities of Sodom and Gomorrah represent frenetic homosexual activity. The word *sodomite*—as derived from the city name of Sodom—has become a word to mean *gay*. However, throughout the Bible, *sodomite* refers to men who are into sex orgies stemming from their exposure to sexually extreme pagan worship practices.

So how did these two towns earn this reputation as gay towns? Were there really two towns full of crazed gay men engaged in raping straight men? How did men who routinely practiced extreme sexual exploitation of others as part of idol worship—who the Bible calls *sodomites*—later become considered to be homosexuals by contemporary Christians?

> Genesis 13:13 (ESV)
>
> Now the people of **Sodom** were wicked, great sinners against the Lord.

> Genesis 18:20-21 (RSV)
>
> Then the Lord said, "Because the outcry against **Sodom and Gomorrah** is great and their sin is very grave, I will go down to see whether they have done altogether according to the outcry which has come to me; and if not, I will know."

So what were the sins of Sodom? Ezekiel lays it out and it's not for being gay:

> Ezekiel 16:49-50 (abridged KJV, ASV, ESV)
>
> Behold, this was the iniquity of your sister **Sodom**:
> -pride,
> -overabundance of food,
> -prosperous ease, and
> -idleness were hers and her daughters;
> -neither did she strengthen the hand of the poor and needy.
> -And they were haughty and committed abominable offenses before me;
> therefore I removed them when I saw it and I saw fit.

But these are the sins of Sodom that the Bible says caused judgment to rained down:

> Jude 1:6-7 (KJV)
>
> And the angels which kept not their first estate, but left their own habitation, he hath reserved in everlasting chains under darkness unto the judgment of the great day. Even as **Sodom**

and Gomorrah, and the cities about them in like manner, **giving themselves over to fornication** (pornography)**, and going after strange flesh** (going sexually after angels), are set forth for an example, suffering the vengeance of eternal fire.

Sodom and Gomorrah suffered the vengeance of eternal fire because their citizens gave themselves over to fornication (sex for the sake of sex that could include what we call rape today and/or sexually extreme pagan worship) AND they went after angels sexually (strange flesh).

The Greek word the Bible uses for *strange flesh* or *other flesh* is **sarkos heteras**. This Greek term has been universally accepted as referring to angels. If the author meant "going after a man" there were many first century Greek words for "man" the author, Jude, could have used. But he didn't.

Here is the whole story that has led some ministers to claim that the men of Sodom were gay. If you actually read it, you can prove to yourself that it is not about gay men.

> Genesis 19:1-14 (NRSV)
>
> The two angels came to Sodom in the evening, and Lot was sitting in the Gateway of Sodom. When Lot saw them, he rose to meet them, and bowed down with his face to the ground.
>
> He said, "Please, my lords, turn aside to your servant's house and spend the night, and wash your feet; then you can rise early and go on your way." They said, "No; we will spend the night in the square."
>
> But he urged him strongly; so they turned aside to him and entered his house; and he made a feast, and baked unleavened bread, and they ate.
>
> But before they lay down, the men of the city, the men of Sodom, both young and old, all the people to the last man, surrounded the house; and they called to Lot, "Where are the

men who came to you tonight? Bring them out to us, so that we may know them."

Lot went out of the door to the men, shut the door after him, and said, "I beg you, my brothers, do not act so wickedly. Look, I have two daughters who have not known a man; let me bring them out to you, and do to them as you please; only do nothing to these men, for they have come under the shelter of my roof."

But they replied, "Stand back!" And they said, "This fellow came here as an alien, and he would play the judge! Now we will deal worse with you than with them." Then they pressed hard against the man Lot, and came near the door to break it down.

But the men (the angels) inside reached out their hands and brought Lot into the house with them, and shut the door. And they struck with blindness the men at the door of the house, both small and great, so that they were unable to find the door.

Then the men (the angels) said to Lot, "Have you anyone else here? Sons-in-law, sons, daughters, or anyone you have in the city bring them out of the place. For we are about to destroy this place, because the outcry against its people has become great before the Lord, and the Lord has sent us to destroy it."

So Lot went out and said to his sons-in-law, who were to marry his daughters, "Up, get out of this place; for the Lord is about destroy the city." But he seemed to his sons-in-law to be jesting.

Observations on this story:

-This story does not describe a raging mob of gay men seeking sex partners. If so, then Lot would not have offered his daughters to them as a substitute for the male guests. He would have offered his future sons-in-law if he wanted to protect the angels.

-In this story, every person in town to the last man was part of this violent mob. It defies reason that there is any city in any place that totally comprises gay men—raging or otherwise.

-What this story clearly describes is gang violence where the mob is seeking victims to brutalize and their choice of brutality, in this story, is through violent sexual humiliation.

Sexual humiliation today, yesterday, and probably tomorrow.

Sodomy is now, and was then, a common form of sexual humiliation between straight men. An example is in the movie *Exodus* from 1960, where the character *Dov Landau* is being questioned by the movie character *Akiva Ben Canaan*.

Dov: What could I do? What can I do?

Akiva: We will take into consideration that you were less than 13 when you went off to Auschwitz. Even so, he must have the truth. Is there anything else?

Dov: Yes.

Akiva: Then tell us.

Dov: No, I won't tell you. Please. Don't make me tell you my... Kill me. I don't care. I won't tell you.

Akiva: Tell us.

Dov: They made me... They...used me...like you use a woman (sob sob).

In this story the young man is describing sexual humiliation at the hands of his Nazi torturers. He is not saying the Nazis were gay. He is saying they were cruel and brutal.

The Bible prophets do not think of Sodom and Gomorrah as gay cities.

Jeremiah 23:14 (NRSV)

But in the prophets of Jerusalem I have seen a more shocking thing. They commit adultery and walk in lies; they strengthened the hands of evildoers, so that no one turns from wickedness; all of them have become like **Sodom** to me, and its inhabitants like **Gomorrah**.

In Biblical times people did not associate Sodom and Gomorrah with homosexuality or even specifically with sexual humiliation. Rather, the sins of Sodom and Gomorrah were general evilness, not caring about others, and being brutal. These were villages where violent criminals ruled.

In 1997, in New York City, Mr. Abner Louima was brutally sodomized in a police department bathroom by three officers with a broomstick. None of the men involved were gay. In October 2008, in New York City, the New York Post reported another brutal police attack on a man who was in police custody and who was sodomized with an object. These attacks were never depicted as gay sex incidents but, rather, rape and torture.

Over human history, military victories have been consummated on the battlefield by the soldiers of the winning army, sodomizing and thereby sexually humiliating and brutalizing the losers. This is a detestable practice that has been documented in many cultures throughout the ages.

Gibeah is proof Sodom's story did not mean homosexuality to people of the Bible.

The story of Gibeah is **the same story** as Sodom. The criminal mob wanted to do its gang-rape style violence on the visiting man and the host protects the visiting guest and offers his daughter and the guest's concubine to the mob instead. The difference is, in this story, the visitor throws his concubine to the gang, who then proceed to rape and kill her.

> Judges 19:22-26 (NRSV)
>
> While they were enjoying themselves, the men of the city, a perverse lot, surrounded the house, and started pounding on the door. They said to the old man, the master of the house, "Bring out the man who came into your house, **so that we may have intercourse with him.**"
>
> And the man, the master of the house, went out to them and said to them, "No, my brothers, do not act so wickedly. Since this man is my guest, do not do this vile thing. Here are my virgin daughter and his concubine; let me bring them out now. Ravage them and do whatever you want to them; but against this man not do such a vile thing."
>
> But the men would not listen to him. So the man seized his concubine, and put her out to them. They wantonly raped her, and abused her all through the night until the morning. And as dawn began to break, they let her go.
>
> As morning appeared, the woman came and fell down at the door of the man's house where her master was, until it was light.

(after more exposition, the story continues)

> Judges 20:4-5 (NRSV)
>
> The Levite, the husband of the woman who was murdered, answered, "I came to Gibeah that belongs to Benjamin, I and my concubine, to spend the night. The lords of Gibeah rose up against me, and surrounded the house at night. **They intended to kill me**, and they raped my concubine until she died."

Observation on this story:

-The violent mob of Gibeah specifically told the visiting man that they wanted to have sexual intercourse with him, but when the man tells the story later he says that they intended to kill him. This clarifies the situation for us today, so we can never interpret this request for intercourse as anything other than a prelude to a violent attack. This is not gay sex. And it was not interpreted as gay sex in Biblical times.

-This is exactly the same scenario that played out with Lot and the angels in Sodom in the book of Genesis.

-The story of Sodom and the story of Gibeah both described gang violence that included male rape as a prelude to murder. Anyone who uses these stories to represent a gay relationship or gay sex would have to add or subtract from the Bible to make their case.

So what is the fate of Sodom?

> Ezekiel 16:53-54 (NRSV)
>
> **I will restore their fortunes**, the fortunes of Sodom and her daughters and the fortunes of Samaria and her daughters, and I will restore your own fortunes along with theirs, in order that you may bear your disgrace and be ashamed of all that you have done, becoming a consolation to them.

Archaeologists have yet to find the burned remains of Sodom and Gomorrah. However, Ezekiel says that God will restore Sodom. So, according to the Bible, the remains of Sodom lie under a current and thriving city—a restored city!

Gay and straight sex is natural.

The Bible uses the word **nature** and **natural** to speak about things that are obvious because they are natural to that person. A natural thing is a physical thing such as one's own body. For example, when the Bible says someone is a *natural Jew*, he is a Jew by birth, not someone who was converted.

Galatians 2:15 (KJV)

We who are Jews **by nature** (The New Living Translations says "You and I are Jews **by birth**"), and not sinners of the Gentiles,

The term *natural* in the scriptures also means something that is instinctual to that person.

Romans 2:14 (KJV)

For when the Gentiles, which have not the law, do **by nature** the things contained in the law, (The New Living Translation says "show that they know this law when they **instinctively** obey it") these, having not the law, are a law unto themselves:

Jude 1:10 (KJV)

But these speak evil of those things which they know not: but what they know **naturally** (the New American Standard Bible says **know by instinct**), as brute beasts, in those things they corrupt themselves.

The term *natural* in the scriptures also means something that is sincere and true for that person.

Philippians 2:20 (KJV)

For I have no man likeminded, who will **naturally** ('**sincerely**' in New King James) care for your state.

So what does this verse mean that has so often been used to claim the Bible is against homosexuals?:

Romans 1:26-27 (KJV)

For this **cause** God gave them up unto vile affections: for even their women did change the **natural** use into that which is **against nature (against their natural inclinations)**: And likewise also the men, **leaving the natural use of the woman** (not limiting themselves to women), burned in their lust one toward another; men with men working that which is unseemly, and receiving in themselves that recompense of their error which was meet.

The *cause* given in the above verse for these unnatural behaviors is that these were people worshiping a deity through sex orgies. It was natural to these people to be straight, but they went against their own nature to engage in same-sex relations.

This is what we see today in the porno industry. The women who are having the "girl-on-girl" porno sessions are not gay. This is straight porn. And the men referenced here, too, are described as those in the throes of orgiastic sex that crosses their natural sexual orientation.

More importantly, Paul expands on his description of these sex addicts that describes a lifestyle of depravity in all their dealings with others that includes every area of their behavior, not just sexual.

If these women referred to in Romans 1:26 - 27 were actually lesbians, then it would be natural for them to have sexual relations with other women. But in the text, the Bible says it was not natural for them, so they were not gay.

The Bible we read today was understood by the Jews and Gentiles of ancient times.

The original Bible scriptures were written by and for the ancient peoples who lived in Biblical times. But now many of the terms in the scriptures have been recently changed in order to advance anti-gay bigotry.

Fornication—*sexually abusing or sexually exploiting another through sex*—has become the vague terms *sexual sin* or *sexual immorality* which is verbal Silly Putty™ to imply homosexuality or almost any other bias held by the reader.

Unnatural—*not native to the sensibilities of a particular person*—has been appropriated by many to mean homosexuality as the biased reader believes same-sex attraction to be universally unnatural.

Sodomy and Sodomites—*male temple prostitutes of the pornographic pagan religions in Bible times*—has been repurposed for decades to mean a homosexual, using the term to erroneously refer to contemporary gay men who are clearly not selling their bodies in the service of extreme sexual pagan worship.

Silly Putty is a trademark owned by Crayola LLC.

The Law - Proof 7

The law is a necessary part of God's message for the sole purpose of stripping it of its power over us.

This book has been loosely structured like a legal brief. There are seven separate arguments to prove that any alleged 'Christian' belief against homosexuality cannot stand up to scripture. Each argument can single-handedly prove the thesis that God is not against gay.

1. The first argument is that God made everything and God made man in his image therefore God is gay which is the same argument for God is black, God is female, and so on as our image is a reflection of God's image. God has many facets and we are all reflections of our Creator.

2. The second argument against anti-gay proselytizing is that it is hypocritical and illogical. The Bible scriptures barely touch upon the subject of what has been interpreted as homosexuality while there is a heavy scriptural focus on behaviors that the Church rarely, if ever, addresses such as adultery and lying. The strength of this argument is that Christ himself was clear that hypocrites are not representing God's intentions.

3. The third argument is that the scriptures are inclusive and, therefore, homosexuals are included in all the blessings and promises in the scriptures. All means all. In fact, male homosexuals were specifically blessed in scripture and their sexual relationships with others was socially accepted and legal at the time the Bible was written.

4. The fourth argument is that we are all scripturally bound by the over-arching Commandment of Love and such a commandment forbids any anti-gay behavior among Christians. The Bible's mandate to love and embrace gay people is as much the Word of God as is John 3:16.

5. The fifth argument is that we do not scripturally have the right to judge anyone, and that includes homosexuals. To take it upon ourselves to say that someone is 'going to Hell' or someone is 'not right with God' is against scripture. We do not have jurisdiction over this matter as only God can legally judge us.

6. The next and most undeniable argument is that the scriptures do not even contain any homosexual references at all — that homosexuality was not at all anything that was thought of in those times as it is thought of today and homosexuality was never anything that was scripturally criticized. There has been a documented corruption of scripture by over-reaching publishers who have promoted a manmade, anti-gay agenda. For example, nowhere in the scriptures does it state that God punished Sodom and Gomorrah for homosexual activity. And Jesus himself addresses the male gay population but only to advise them to not enter into marriage with women (Matthew 19:9 - 12).

7. This chapter you are reading now is the last argument, number seven. If there is anyone who is not persuaded by the first six arguments and who is still confident that, somehow, being gay is against God's divine order and that, somehow, some <u>supposedly</u> anti-gay scriptures prove God is against homosexuality, then this chapter is the last argument in this legal brief. It is about the law. Anyone who is clinging to the idea that homosexuality is against God's Law will learn that we are freed of the law by the sacrifice of Jesus who came to save us all from the law. So this is the last argument. There is no law.

There is no law because of Jesus.

Jesus died to free us from the law.

If we could keep the law—if we could be perfect—then Jesus died for no reason. If we could be perfect and if we could obey all the rules set down by Moses, then Jesus didn't have to die. We would not have to be "saved" by anyone. We could just keep the law and behave ourselves. Easy.

But the point of the law is that we cannot keep it. I don't care who you are, you cannot ever, ever, ever, ever keep the law. Paraphrasing Isaiah 64:6, we are a mess and all our efforts to be "good" are like garbage to God. So that's why we needed Jesus. We had to be saved from this legalistic system that no one can ever maintain.

> **The law is important because it is the picture of foolish man thinking that he could be perfect like God.**

What we think of as the law came through Moses, the 'Law of Sin and Death.' That all started when Moses asked God to give him all the laws and statutes (as if one could codify God into a set a rules like software).

The result was the Law of Sin and Death in which the violation of almost any law or statute was punishable by death. So, before the law was given, if someone violated the Sabbath, they were just reminded as a correction (Exodus 16:27, *people violated the Sabbath without consequences*). After the law was given from Mount Zion, the same behavior was punishable by death (Exodus 31:14, *a violation of the Sabbath is now punished by death*).

The law was not God's idea. It was man's idea. Before the law was given, people would ask God questions and he would answer on a case-by-case basis. There was no cookie-cutter response. God's people would complain to God about this or that and even break the Sabbath and no one died. But when these complaining, disobedient people told Moses that they **would** obey God, that they **will do all that God has spoken** (Exodus 19:8), things changed.

Exodus 19:8 (KJV)

And all the people answered together, and said, **All that the Lord hath spoken we will do**. And Moses returned the words of the people unto the Lord.

The shock of this statement is that it was given in the third month of the Israelites walking in the wilderness after escaping Egypt. In that short period of time, the Bible recounts that the Israelites were repeatedly unable to obey Moses even though he spoke in the name of God. When Moses told them to listen to him because God told him he would take them out of Egypt, the people grumbled and wouldn't listen to Moses.

> Exodus 6:9 (KJV)
>
> And Moses spake so unto the children of Israel: but **they hearkened not unto Moses** for anguish of spirit, and for cruel bondage.

> Exodus 15:24 (KJV)
>
> **And the people murmured against Moses**, saying, What shall we drink?.

> Exodus 16:2 (KJV)
>
> And the whole congregation of the children of **Israel murmured against Moses** and Aaron in the wilderness

> Exodus 16:7 (KJV)
>
> ...for that he heareth **your murmurings against the Lord**: and what are we, that ye murmur against us?

> Exodus 16:8 (KJV)
>
> ...for that the Lord **heareth your murmurings** which ye murmur against him: and what are we? your murmurings are not against us, but against the Lord.

> Exodus 16:9 (KJV)
>
> And Moses spake unto Aaron, Say unto all the congregation of the children of Israel, Come near before the Lord: **for he hath heard your murmurings**.

> Exodus 16:11-12 (KJV)
>
> And the Lord spake unto Moses, saying, I have heard the murmurings of the children of Israel...

But God took care of the Israelites, whether they were obedient or not.

> Exodus 16:4 (KJV)
>
> Then said the Lord unto Moses, Behold, I will rain bread from heaven for you; and the people shall go out and gather a certain rate every day, that I may prove them, **whether they will walk in my law, or no**.

Even when they deliberately disobeyed God's law of keeping the Sabbath, there were no consequences for the Israelites.

> Exodus 16: 19-20 (KJV)
>
> And Moses said, **Let no man leave of it till the morning. Notwithstanding they hearkened not unto Moses;** but some of them left of it until the morning, and it bred worms, and stank: and Moses was wroth with them.

> Exodus 16:25-29 (KJV)
>
> **And Moses said,** Eat that to day; **for to day is a sabbath unto the Lord:** to day ye shall not find it in the field. Six days ye shall gather it; but on the seventh day, which is the sabbath, in it there shall be none. **And it came to pass, that there went out some of the people on the seventh day for to gather,** and they found none. And the Lord said unto Moses, **How long refuse ye to keep my commandments and my laws? See, for that the Lord hath given you the sabbath,** therefore he giveth you on the sixth day the bread of two days; abide ye every man in his place, **let no man go out of his place on the seventh day**.

So Moses was teaching God's law out there in the desert and nobody died when they disobeyed. The people came to Moses for this instruction, and the Israelites were learning God's law and sometimes they obeyed and sometimes not and no one died when they slipped up.

But then, one day the Israelites said they would DO all the laws. THAT changed everything. Only three months into their freedom from their Egyptian masters, the Israelites changed their response to God and that changed their relationship to God for the next 1500 years.

What happened? The Israelites claimed they were able to be perfect, able to conform to all the laws! In other words, they were able to be like God. Crazy, right?

First, God said something to them that he had said before and said often:

> Exodus 19:5 (KJV)
>
> Now therefore, **if ye will obey my voice indeed, and keep my covenant**, then ye shall be a peculiar treasure unto me above all people: for all the earth is mine

God had said this before to the Israelites. But this time they responded in a new way:

> Exodus 19:8 (KJV)
>
> And all the people answered together, and said, **All that the Lord hath spoken we will do.** And Moses returned the words of the people unto the Lord.

What? They said they will do all that God tells them to do? What? They said they will obey God's voice and keep his covenant? What? They have never said that before.

These are a people that had so many quarrels among themselves that it wore out Moses and he had to put in place 70 people to help him parse through the complaints they lodged against each other daily. So, for these people with these daily habits of abusing each other, to then state that they will be able to, 100%, do everything that God says to do — well, that was ridiculous. If that were true, then making DEATH the consequence for disobedience was not a problem since they all said they will, 100%, do everything that God said, right?

So the law had to be put in place to make the point that we can never depend on ourselves. We cannot do anything, much less everything.

We needed Jesus to save us from that thinking so we can have the freedom to be wholly dependent on God's love for everything.

God then gave Moses the Ten Commandments. Then Moses took it upon himself to add over 600 more laws with consequences for disobediance.

After that statement by the Israelites, after anyone broke the law, the consequence was usually DEATH. If someone didn't keep the Sabbeth, DEATH. If anyone was disrespectful to his parents, DEATH.

Now we have the Law of Sin and Death. Now we HAVE to be saved. We have to be saved from thinking we could ever be perfect. We have to be saved by Jesus.

Binary thinking like the law is very robotic. The Mosaic Law was a code that detailed what you needed to do or not do to be perfect. Off/On. It was an attractive but unrealistic idea that it was possible to keep the law and to then be perfect.

But it is not possible.

> **So God gave us the law to make a point that we cannot keep the law.**

In the Bible, the law was an example of a perfect thing. It has been described as 'majestic.' It could not be modified or softened for anyone.

Luke 16:16-17 (NRSV)

The law and the prophets were in effect until John came; since then the good news of the kingdom of God is proclaimed, and everyone tries to enter it by force. **But it is easier for heaven and earth to pass away, than for one stroke of a letter in the law to be dropped.**

In the Bible, the law represented perfection. The only way one could keep the law was to keep it all.

James 2:10-11 (NRSV)

For whoever keeps the whole law but fails in one point have become accountable for all of it. For the one who said, "You shall not commit adultery," also said, "You shall not murder." Now if you do not commit adultery but if you murder, you have become a transgressor of the law.

The law was like computer software. Computer logic is perfect and inflexible. To violate any part of computer logic would corrupt the entire program. So if you violated one part of the law, you have ruined the perfection of the law. You have sullied its majesty.

The Bible rules are broken by all the patriarchs.

In the Bible we see example after example of famous, Godly, important men who were unable to keep the law. Important Jewish leaders who knew the law were always stubbing their toes on it because they were trying to become righteous through works.

Romans 9:30-33 (NRSV)

What then are we to say? Gentiles, who did not strive for righteousness, have attained it, that is, righteousness through faith, **but Israel, who did strive for the righteousness that is based on the law, did not succeed in fulfilling that law. Why not? Because they did not strive for it on the basis of faith, but as if it were based on works.** They have stumbled over the stumbling stone, as it is written, "See, I'm laying in Zion a stone that will make people stumble, a rock that will make them fall, and whoever believes in him will not be put to shame."

Moses told lies (Exodus 5:1). Abraham told lies (Genesis 20) and married his father's daughter, his half-sister, although the law said not to (Leviticus 18:9). Jacob married four sisters, all daughters of Laban, although the law forbid marrying sisters (Leviticus 18:18). Judah disobeyed the law to provide his daughter-in-law with a replacement husband (Genesis 38:1-11) and this legal lapse led to the birth of an illegitimate child, which was improper by Jewish Law (Deuteronomy 23:2). God ordered Hosea to marry a prostitute (Hosea 1:2) which was not permitted to holy men (Leviticus 21:13). And David committed adultery (2 Samuel 11:2-5) and tacitly committed murder to cover it up (2 Samuel 11:14-17). I'm just skimming, of course.

The history of the law.

Because the Bible is a large collection of books that God inspired through a succession of authors, it has been tempting for people to focus on single phrases, certain verses, and to not see the messages that are only explained through embracing the entire Bible as a whole. To not embrace the entire Bible is to be disobedient.

> Deuteronomy 4: 2 (NRSV)
>
> You must neither add anything to what I command you **nor take away anything from it**, but keep the commandments of the Lord your God with which I am charging you.

Deuteronomy is only the sixth book written in what is now the Bible. When Moses wrote this, he may not have realized there were 60 more books to come. But God knew. He knew the end from the beginning and the entire story arc that will be written down over the next almost 1600 years. Is God speaking through Deuteronomy? Yes. Is God still speaking through the rest of the Bible? Yes.

Would you leave 10 minutes into a movie and believe that you got the entire story of the movie? You wouldn't. The verse above is God saying, early in his Book, "Hang in there and read all the way through this Book. It will be important."

Here below are periods of time in the Bible and the role the law played in all these time periods. It is clear from the chart below that the law was a temporary situation that was put in place for a specific set of circumstances, as a lesson that we all can learn now, that the law was not God's original plan.

Adam—1675 years
God speaks directly to man and has one law, don't eat from the tree

Noah—233 years
God speaks directly to man, no laws.

Abraham—430 years
God speaks directly to man. God gives His promise to Abraham and no laws

Moses—1547 years
God speaks to prophets; the High Priest represents the people to God; The law is given.

THE LAW

Christ—2000+ years
God speaks directly to man again; the Law is fulfilled and finished

From the timeline we see that there was over 2000 years of God speaking directly to man and no formalized laws before Moses. And we see that there has now been more than 2000 years since Christ and his fulfillment of the law.

So the time of the law was a departure from God's original plan and we are now in the post-law world.

All the time periods in this graphic can be described by the scriptures in Romans 5:12 - 14; 18 - 21:

> Romans 5:12-14; 18-21 (NRSV)
>
> **(Adam's time)** Therefore, just as sin came into the world through one man, and death came through sin, and so death spread to all because all have sinned – sin was indeed in the world before the law, but sin is not reckoned when there is no law.
>
> **(Moses' time)** Yet death exercised dominion from Adam to Moses, even over those whose sins were not like the transgression of Adam, who is a type of the one who was to come.
>
> **(Christ's time)** Therefore just as one man's trespass (Adam) led to condemnation for all, so one man's act of righteousness (Jesus) leads to justification and life for all. For just as by the one man's disobedience (Adam) many were made sinners, so by the one man's obedience (Jesus) the many will be made righteous.
>
> **(Moses' time)** But law came in, with the result that the trespass multiplied;
>
> **(Christ's time)** But where sin increased, grace abounded all the more, so that, just as sin exercised dominion in death (in the time of Moses), so grace might also exercise dominion to justification leading to eternal life to Jesus Christ our Lord (in the time of Jesus which is now and forever).

First there was only ONE law:

One Law

Genesis 3:3 (KJV) In the Garden

But of the fruit of the tree which is in the midst of the garden, God hath said, Ye shall not eat of it, neither shall ye touch it, lest ye die.

Then God gave us Ten laws:

Ten Laws

Exodus 20:1-17; Deuteronomy 5:4-21 (NKJV)
The 'Ten Commandments'

1. You shall have no other gods before me.

2. You shall not make for yourself a carved image, or any likeness of anything that is in heaven above, or that is in the earth beneath, or that is in the water under the earth. You shall not bow down to them nor serve them, for I the LORD your God am a jealous God, visiting the iniquity of the fathers on the children to the third and the fourth generation of those who hate me, but showing steadfast love to thousands of those who love me and keep my commandments.

3. You shall not take the name of the LORD your God in vain, for the LORD will not hold him guiltless who takes his name in vain.

4. Remember the Sabbath day, to keep it holy. Six days you shall labor, and do all your work, but the seventh day is a Sabbath to the LORD your God. On it you shall not do any work, you, or your son, or your daughter, your male servant, or your female servant, or your livestock, or the sojourner who is within your gates. For in six days the LORD made heaven and earth, the sea, and all that is in them, and rested

on the seventh day. Therefore the LORD blessed the Sabbath day and made it holy.

5. Honor your father and your mother, that your days may be long in the land that the LORD your God is giving you.

6. You shall not murder.

7. You shall not commit adultery.

8. You shall not steal.

9. You shall not bear false witness against your neighbor.

10. You shall not covet your neighbor's house; you shall not covet your neighbor's wife, or his male servant, or his female servant, or his ox, or his donkey, or anything that is your neighbor's.

Then Moses gave us more laws—with consequences:

Six Hundred Thirteen Laws

The Mosaic Laws – Man endeavoring to codify all the ritualistic religious traditions of being Jewish in those times.*

1 To know there is a God Ex. 20:2
2 Not to entertain thoughts of other gods besides Him Ex. 20:3
3 To know that He is one Deut. 6:4
4 To love Him Deut. 6:5
5 To fear Him Deut. 10:20
6 To sanctify His Name Lev. 22:32
7 Not to profane His Name Lev. 22:32
8 Not to destroy objects associated with His Name Deut. 12:4
9 To listen to the prophet speaking in His Name Deut. 18:15
10 Not to test the prophet unduly Deut. 6:16

Laws of Character

11 To emulate His ways Deut. 28:9

12 To cleave to those who know Him Deut. 10:20

13 To love Jews Lev. 19:18

14 To love converts Deut. 10:19

15 Not to hate fellow Jews Lev. 19:17

16 To reprove Lev. 19:17

17 Not to embarrass others Lev. 19:17

18 Not to oppress the weak Ex. 21:22

19 Not to speak derogatorily of others Lev. 19:16

20 Not to take revenge Lev. 19:18

21 Not to bear a grudge Lev. 19:18

Laws of Torah Study

22 To learn Torah Deut. 6:7

23 To honor those who teach and know Torah Lev. 19:32

Laws of Idolatry and Paganism

24 Not to inquire into idolatry Lev. 19:4

25 Not to follow the whims of your heart or what your eyes see Num. 15:39

26 Not to blaspheme Ex. 22:27

27 Not to worship idols in the manner they are worshiped Ex. 20:5

28 Not to worship idols in the four ways we worship God Ex. 20:5

29 Not to make an idol for yourself Ex. 20:4

30 Not to make an idol for others Lev. 19:4

31 Not to make human forms even for decorative purposes Ex. 20:20

32 Not to turn a city to idolatry Ex. 23:13

33 To burn a city that has turned to idol worship Deut. 13:17

34 Not to rebuild it as a city Deut. 13:17

35 Not to derive benefit from it Deut. 13:18

36 Not to missionize an individual to idol worship Deut. 13:12

37 Not to love the missionary Deut. 13:9

38 Not to cease hating the missionary Deut. 13:9

39 Not to save the missionary Deut. 13:9

40 Not to say anything in his defense Deut. 13:9

41 Not to refrain from incriminating him Deut. 13:9

42 Not to prophesize in the name of idolatry Deut. 13:14

43 Not to listen to a false prophet Deut. 13:4

44 Not to prophesize falsely in the name of God Deut. 18:20

45 Not to be afraid of killing the false prophet Deut. 18:22

46 Not to swear in the name of an idol Ex. 23:13

47 Not to perform ov (medium) Lev. 19:31

48 Not to perform yidoni (magical seer) Lev. 19:31

49 Not to pass your children through the fire to Molech Lev. 18:21

50 Not to erect a column in a public place of worship Deut. 16:22

51 Not to bow down on smooth stone Lev. 26:1

52 Not to plant a tree in the Temple courtyard Deut. 16:21

53 To destroy idols and their accessories Deut. 12:2

54 Not to derive benefit from idols and their accessories Deut. 7:26

55 Not to derive benefit from ornaments of idols Deut. 7:25

56 Not to make a covenant with idolaters Deut. 7:2

57 Not to show favor to them Deut. 7:2

58 Not to let them dwell in our land Ex. 23:33

59 Not to imitate them in customs and clothing Lev. 20:23

60 Not to be superstitious Lev. 19:26

61 Not to go into a trance to foresee events, etc. Deut. 18:10

62 Not to engage in astrology Lev. 19:26

63 Not to mutter incantations Deut. 18:11

64 Not to attempt to contact the dead Deut. 18:11

65 Not to consult the ov (ghosts or demons) Deut. 18:11

66 Not to consult the yidoni (spiritualists) Deut. 18:11

67 Not to perform acts of magic Deut. 18:10

68 Men must not shave the hair off the sides of their head Lev. 19:27

69 Men must not shave their beards with a razor Lev. 19:27

70 Men must not wear women's clothing Deut. 22:5

71 Women must not wear men's clothing Deut. 22:5

72 Not to tattoo the skin Lev. 19:28

73 Not to tear the skin in mourning Deut. 14:1

74 Not to make a bald spot in mourning Deut. 14:1

Law of Repentance

75 To repent and confess wrongdoings Num. 5:7

Law of Reading the Shema

76 To say the Shema twice daily Deut. 6:7

Laws of Prayer and Kohanic Blessings

77 To serve the Almighty with prayer daily Ex. 23:25

78 The Kohanim must bless the Jewish nation daily Num. 6:23

Laws of Tefillin, Mezuza and Sefer Torah

79 To wear tefillin on the head Deut. 6:8

80 To bind tefillin on the arm Deut. 6:8

81 To put a mezuzah on each door post Deut. 6:9

82 Each male must write a Sefer Torah Deut. 31:19

83 The king must have a separate Sefer Torah for himself Deut. 17:18

Law of Tzitzit

84 To have tzitzit (tassels) on four-cornered garments Num. 15:38

Law of Blessings

85 To bless the Almighty after eating Deut. 8:10

Law of Circumcision

86 To circumcise all males on the eighth day after their birth Lev. 12:3

Laws of the Sabbath

87 To rest on the seventh day Ex. 23:12

88 Not to do prohibited labor on the seventh day Ex. 20:10

89 The court must not inflict punishment on Shabbat Ex. 35:3

90 Not to walk outside the city boundary on Shabbat Ex. 16:29

91 To sanctify the day with Kiddush and Havdallah Ex. 20:8

Laws of Yom Kippur Rest

92 To rest from prohibited labor Lev. 23:32

93 Not to do prohibited labor on Yom Kippur Lev. 23:32

94 To afflict yourself on Yom Kippur Lev. 16:29

95 Not to eat or drink on Yom Kippur Lev. 23:29

Laws of Festival Rest

96 To rest on the first day of Passover Lev. 23:7

97 Not to do prohibited labor on the first day of Passover Lev. 23:8

98 To rest on the seventh day of Passover Lev. 23:8

99 Not to do prohibited labor on the seventh day of Passover Lev. 23:8

100 To rest on Shavuot Lev. 23:21

101 Not to do prohibited labor on Shavuot Lev. 23:21

102 To rest on Rosh Hashana Lev. 23:24

103 Not to do prohibited labor on Rosh Hashana Lev. 23:25

104 To rest on Sukkot Lev. 23:35

105 Not to do prohibited labor on Sukkot Lev. 23:35

106 To rest on Shmini Atzeret Lev. 23:36

107 Not to do prohibited labor on Shmini Atzeret Lev. 23:36

Laws of Chometz and Matzah

108 Not to eat chametz on the afternoon of the 14th day of Nissan Deut. 16:3

109 To destroy all chametz on 14th day of Nissan Ex. 12:15

110 Not to eat chametz all seven days of Passover Ex. 13:3

111 Not to eat mixtures containing chametz all seven days of Passover Ex. 12:20

112 Not to see chametz in your domain seven days Ex. 13:7

113 Not to find chametz in your domain seven days Ex. 12:19

114 To eat matzah on the first night of Passover Ex. 12:18

115 To relate the exodus from Egypt on that night Ex. 13:8

Laws of Shofar, Sukkah, Lulav

116 To hear the Shofar on the first day of Tishrei (Rosh Hashana) Num. 29:1

117 To dwell in a Sukkah for the seven days of Sukkot Lev. 23:42

118 To take up a Lulav and Etrog all seven days Lev. 23:40

Law of Shekalim

119 Each man must give a half shekel annually Ex. 30:13

Law of Sanctification of Months

120 Courts must calculate to determine when a new month begins Ex. 12:2

Law of Fasts

121 To afflict and cry out before God in times of catastrophe Num. 10:9

Laws of Marriage

122 To marry a wife by means of ketubah and kiddushin Deut. 22:13

123 Not to have relations with women not thus married Deut. 23:18

124 Not to withhold food, clothing, and relations from your wife Ex. 21:10

125 To have children with one's wife Gen 1:28

Laws of Divorce

126 To issue a divorce by means of a "get" document Deut. 24:1

127 A man must not remarry his wife after she has married someone else Deut. 24:4

Laws of Yivum and Chalitzah (Levirate Marriage)

128 To do yibum (marry childless brother's widow) Deut. 25:5

129 To do chalitzah (freeing a widow from yibum) Deut. 25:9

130 The widow must not remarry until the ties with her brother-in-law are removed Deut. 25:5

Laws of Women

131 A man must pay the bride-price if he takes a maiden Ex. 22:16

132 The man must marry the maiden he took (if she chooses) Deut. 22:29

133 He is not allowed to divorce her Deut. 22:29

134 If a man falsely claims bride was not a maiden, he can never divorce her Deut. 22:19

135 He must not divorce her Deut. 22:19

Laws of Sotah (Suspect Wife)

136 To fulfill the laws of the Sotah Num. 5:30

137 Not to put oil on her meal offering Num. 5:15

138 Not to put frankincense on her meal offering Num. 5:15

Laws of Forbidden Relations

139 Not to have sexual relations with your mother Lev. 18:7

140 Not to have sexual relations with your father's wife Lev. 18:8

141 Not to have sexual relations with your sister Lev. 18:9

142 Not to have sexual relations with your father's wife's daughter Lev. 18:11

143 Not to have sexual relations with your son's daughter Lev. 18:10

144 Not to have sexual relations with your daughter Lev. 18:10

145 Not to have sexual relations with your daughter's daughter Lev. 18:10

146 Not to have sexual relations with a woman and her daughter Lev. 18:17

147 Not to have sexual relations with a woman and her son's daughter Lev. 18:17

148 Not to have sexual relations with a woman and her daughter's daughter Lev. 18:17

149 Not to have sexual relations with your father's sister Lev. 18:12

150 Not to have sexual relations with your mother's sister Lev. 18:13

151 Not to have sexual relations with your father's brother's wife Lev. 18:14

152 Not to have sexual relations with your son's wife Lev. 18:15

153 Not to have sexual relations with your brother's wife Lev. 18:16

154 Not to have sexual relations with your wife's sister Lev. 18:18

155 A man must not have sexual relations with a beast Lev. 18:23

156 A woman must not have sexual relations with a beast Lev. 18:23

157 A man must not have sexual relations with a man Lev. 18:22, Lev. 20:13

158 Not to have sexual relations with your mother Lev. 18:7

159 Not to have sexual relations with your aunt Lev. 18:14

160 Not to have sexual relations with a married woman Lev. 18:20

161 Not to have sexual relations with a menstrually impure woman Lev. 18:19

162 Not to marry non-Jews Deut. 7:3

163 Not to let Moabite and Ammonite males marry into the Jewish people Deut. 23:3

164 Don't keep a third generation Egyptian convert from marrying into the Jewish people Deut. 23:7-8

165 Not to refrain from marrying a third generation Edomite convert Deut. 23:7-8

166 Not to let a mamzer marry into the Jewish people Deut. 23:2

167 Not to let a castrated man marry into the Jewish people Deut. 23:1

168 Not to castrate any male (including animals) Lev. 22:24

169 The High Priest must not marry a widow Lev. 21:14

170 The High Priest must not have sexual relations with a widow even outside of marriage Lev. 21:15

171 The High Priest must marry a virgin maiden Lev. 21:13

172 A Kohen must not marry a divorcee Lev. 21:7

173 A Kohen must not marry a zonah (a woman who had forbidden relations) Lev. 21:7

174 A priest must not marry a chalalah (party to or product of 169-172) Lev. 21:7

175 Not to make pleasurable contact with any forbidden woman Lev. 18:6

Laws of Forbidden Foods

176 To examine the signs of animals to distinguish between kosher and non-kosher Lev. 11:2

177 To examine the signs of fowl to distinguish between kosher and non-kosher Deut. 14:11

178 To examine the signs of fish to distinguish between kosher and non-kosher Lev. 11:9

179 To examine the signs of locusts to distinguish between kosher and non-kosher Lev. 11:21

180 Not to eat non-kosher animals Lev. 11:4

181 Not to eat non-kosher fowl Lev. 11:13

182 Not to eat non-kosher fish Lev. 11:11

183 Not to eat non-kosher flying insects Deut. 14:19

184 Not to eat non-kosher creatures that crawl on land Lev. 11:41

185 Not to eat non-kosher maggots Lev. 11:44

186 Not to eat worms found in fruit on the ground Lev. 11:42

187 Not to eat creatures that live in water other than fish Lev. 11:43

188 Not to eat the meat of an animal that died without ritual slaughter Deut. 14:21

189 Not to benefit from an ox condemned to be stoned Ex. 21:28

190 Not to eat meat of an animal that was mortally wounded Ex. 22:30

191 Not to eat a limb torn off a living creature Deut. 12:23

192 Not to eat blood Lev. 3:17

193 Not to eat certain fats of clean animals Lev. 3:17

194 Not to eat the sinew of the thigh Gen. 32:33

195 Not to eat meat and milk cooked together Ex. 23:19

196 Not to cook meat and milk together Ex. 34:26

197 Not to eat bread from new grain before the Omer Lev. 23:14

198 Not to eat parched grains from new grain before the Omer Lev. 23:14

199 Not to eat ripened grains from new grain before the Omer Lev. 23:14

200 Not to eat fruit of a tree during its first three years Lev. 19:23

201 Not to eat diverse seeds planted in a vineyard Deut. 22:9

202 Not to eat untithed fruits Lev. 22:15

203 Not to drink wine poured in service to idols Deut. 32:38

Laws of Slaughtering

204 To ritually slaughter an animal before eating it Deut. 12:21

205 Not to slaughter an animal and its offspring on the same day Lev. 22:28

206 To cover the blood (of a slaughtered beast or fowl) with earth Lev. 17:13

207 Not to take the mother bird from her children Deut. 22:6

208 To release the mother bird if she was taken from the nest Deut. 22:7

Laws of Oaths

209 Not to swear falsely in God's Name Lev. 19:12

210 Not to take God's Name in vain Ex. 20:7

211 Not to deny possession of something entrusted to you Lev. 19:11

212 Not to swear in denial of a monetary claim Lev. 19:11

213 To swear in God's Name to confirm the truth when deemed necessary by court Deut. 10:20

Laws of Vows

214 To fulfill what was uttered and to do what was avowed Deut. 23:24

215 Not to break oaths or vows Num. 30:3

216 For oaths and vows annulled, there are the laws of annulling vows explicit in the Torah Num. 30:3

Laws of The Nazir

217 The Nazir must let his hair grow Num. 6:5

218 He must not cut his hair Num. 6:5

219 He must not drink wine, wine mixtures, or wine vinegar Num. 6:3

220 He must not eat fresh grapes Num. 6:3

221 He must not eat raisins Num. 6:3

222 He must not eat grape seeds Num. 6:4

223 He must not eat grape skins Num. 6:4

224 He must not be under the same roof as a corpse Num. 6:6

225 He must not come into contact with the dead Num. 6:7

226 He must shave after bringing sacrifices upon completion of his Nazirite period Num. 6:9

Laws of Estimated Values and Vows

227 To estimate the value of people as determined by the Torah Lev. 27:2

228 To estimate the value of consecrated animals Lev. 27:12-13

229 To estimate the value of consecrated houses Lev. 27:14

230 To estimate the value of consecrated fields Lev. 27:16

231 Carry out the laws of interdicting possessions (cherem) Lev. 27:28

232 Not to sell the cherem Lev. 27:28

233 Not to redeem the cherem Lev. 27:28

Laws of Mixed Species

234 Not to plant diverse seeds together Lev. 19:19

235 Not to plant grains or greens in a vineyard Deut. 22:9

236 Not to crossbreed animals Lev. 19:19

237 Not to work different animals together Deut. 22:10

238 Not to wear sha'atnez, a cloth woven of wool and linen Deut. 22:11

Laws of Gifts to the Poor

239 To leave a corner of the field uncut for the poor Lev. 19:10

240 Not to reap that corner Lev. 19:9

241 To leave gleanings Lev. 19:9

242 Not to gather the gleanings Lev. 19:9

243 To leave the gleanings of a vineyard Lev. 19:10

244 Not to gather the gleanings of a vineyard Lev. 19:10

245 To leave the unformed clusters of grapes Lev. 19:10

246 Not to pick the unformed clusters of grapes Lev. 19:10

247 To leave the forgotten sheaves in the field Deut. 24:19

248 Not to retrieve them Deut. 24:19

249 To separate the tithe for the poor Deut. 14:28

250 To give charity Deut. 15:8

251 Not to withhold charity from the poor Deut. 15:7

252 To set aside Trumah Gedolah (tithe for the Kohen) Deut. 18:4

253 The Levite must set aside a tenth of his tithe Num. 18:26

254 Not to preface one tithe to the next, but separate them in their proper order Ex. 22:28

255 A non-Kohen must not eat Trumah Lev. 22:10

256 A hired worker or a Jewish bondsman of a Kohen must not eat Trumah Lev. 22:10

257 An uncircumcised Kohen must not eat Trumah Ex.12:48

258 An impure Kohen must not eat Trumah Lev. 22:4

259 A chalalah must not eat Trumah Lev. 22:12

Law of Ma'aser

260 To set aside Ma'aser each planting year and give it to a Levite Num. 18:24

Laws of The Second Tithe and Fourth Year Produce

261 To set aside the second tithe (Ma'aser Sheni) Deut. 14:22

262 Not to spend its redemption money on anything but food, drink, or ointment Deut. 26:14

263 Not to eat Ma'aser Sheni while impure Deut. 26:14

264 A mourner on the first day after death must not eat Ma'aser Sheni Deut. 26:14

265 Not to eat Ma'aser Sheni grains outside Jerusalem Deut. 12:17

266 Not to eat Ma'aser Sheni wine products outside Jerusalem Deut. 12:17

267 Not to eat Ma'aser Sheni oil outside Jerusalem Deut. 12:17

268 The fourth year crops must be totally for holy purposes like Ma'aser Sheni Lev. 19:24

269 To read the confession of tithes every fourth and seventh year Deut. 26:13

Laws of First Fruits and other Kohanic Gifts

270 To set aside the first fruits and bring them to the Temple Ex. 23:19

271 The Kohanim must not eat the first fruits outside Jerusalem Deut. 12:17

272 To read the Torah portion pertaining to their presentation Deut. 26:5

273 To set aside a portion of dough for a Kohen Num. 15:20

274 To give the shoulder, two cheeks, and stomach of slaughtered animals to a Kohen Deut. 18:3

275 To give the first sheering of sheep to a Kohen Deut. 18:4

276 To redeem the firstborn sons and give the money to a Kohen Num. 18:15

277 To redeem the firstborn donkey by giving a lamb to a Kohen Ex. 13:13

278 To break the neck of the donkey if the owner does not intend to redeem it Ex. 13:13

Laws of The Sabbatical and Jubilee Years

279 To rest the land during the seventh year by not doing any work which enhances growth Ex. 34:21

280 Not to work the land during the seventh year Lev. 25:4

281 Not to work with trees to produce fruit during that year Lev. 25:4

282 Not to reap crops that grow wild that year in the normal manner Lev. 25:5

283 Not to gather grapes which grow wild that year in the normal way Lev. 25:5

284 To leave free all produce which grew in that year Ex. 23:11

285 To release all loans during the seventh year Deut. 15:2

286 Not to pressure or claim from the borrower Deut. 15:2

287 Not to refrain from lending immediately before the release of the loans for fear of monetary loss Deut. 15:9

288 The Sanhedrin must count seven groups of seven years Lev. 25:8

289 The Sanhedrin must sanctify the fiftieth year Lev. 25:10

290 To blow the Shofar on the tenth of Tishrei to free the slaves Lev. 25:9

291 Not to work the soil during the fiftieth year Lev. 25:11

292 Not to reap in the normal manner that which grows wild in the fiftieth year Lev. 25:11

293 Not to pick grapes which grew wild in the normal manner in the fiftieth year Lev. 25:11

294 Carry out the laws of sold family properties Lev. 25:24

295 Not to sell the land in Israel indefinitely Lev. 25:23

296 Carry out the laws of houses in walled cities Lev. 25:29

297 The Tribe of Levi must not be given a portion of the land in Israel, rather they are given cities to dwell in Deut. 18:1

298 The Levites must not take a share in the spoils of war Deut. 18:1

299 To give the Levites cities to inhabit and their surrounding fields Num. 35:2

300 Not to sell the fields but they shall remain the Levites' before and after the Jubilee year Lev. 25:34

Laws of The Temple

301 To build a Sanctuary Ex. 25:8

302 Not to build the altar with stones hewn by metal Ex. 20:22

303 Not to climb steps to the altar Ex. 20:23

304 To show reverence to the Temple Lev. 1930

305 To guard the Temple area Num. 18:2

306 Not to leave the Temple unguarded Num. 18:5

Laws of Temple Vessels and Employees

307 To prepare the anointing oil Ex. 30:31

308 Not to reproduce the anointing oil Ex. 30:32

309 Not to anoint with anointing oil Ex. 30:32

310 Not to reproduce the incense formula Ex. 30:37

311 Not to burn anything on the Golden Altar besides incense Ex. 30:9

312 The Levites must transport the ark on their shoulders Num. 7:9

313 Not to remove the staves from the ark Ex. 25:15

314 The Levites must work in the Temple Num. 18:23

315 No Levite must do another's work of either a Kohen or a Levite Num. 18:3

316 To dedicate the Kohen for service Lev. 21:8

317 The kohanic work shifts must be equal during holidays Deut. 18:6-8

318 The Kohanim must wear their priestly garments during service Ex. 28:2

319 Not to tear the priestly garments Ex. 28:32

320 The breastplate must not be loosened from the Efode Ex. 28:28

Laws of Entering the Temple

321 A Kohen must not enter the Temple intoxicated Lev. 10:9

322 A Kohen must not enter the Temple with long hair Lev. 10:6

323 A Kohen must not enter the Temple with torn clothes Lev. 10:6

324 A Kohen must not enter the Temple indiscriminately Lev. 16:2

325 A Kohen must not leave the Temple during service Lev. 10:7

326 To send the impure from the Temple Num. 5:2

327 Impure people must not enter the Temple Num. 5:3

328 Impure people must not enter the Temple Mount area Deut. 23:11

329 Impure Kohanim must not do service in the temple Lev. 22:2

330 An impure Kohen, following immersion, must wait until after sundown before returning to service Lev. 22:7

331 A Kohen must wash his hands and feet before service Ex. 30:19

332 A Kohen with a physical blemish must not enter the sanctuary or approach the altar Lev. 21:23

333 A Kohen with a physical blemish must not serve Lev.21:17

334 A Kohen with a temporary blemish must not serve Lev. 21:17

335 One who is not a Kohen must not serve Num. 18:4

Laws of Restrictions Concerning Sacrifices

336 To offer only unblemished animals Lev. 22:21

337 Not to dedicate a blemished animal for the altar Lev. 22:20

338 Not to slaughter it Lev. 22:22

339 Not to sprinkle its blood Lev. 22:24

340 Not to burn its fat Lev. 22:22

341 Not to offer a temporarily blemished animal Deut. 17:1

342 Not to sacrifice blemished animals even if offered by non-Jews Lev. 22:25

343 Not to inflict wounds upon dedicated animals Lev. 22:21

344 To redeem dedicated animals which have become disqualified Deut. 12:15

345 To offer only animals which are at least eight days old Lev. 22:27

346 Not to offer animals bought with the wages of a harlot or the animal exchanged for a dog Deut. 23:19

347 Not to burn honey or yeast on the altar Lev. 2:11

348 To salt all sacrifices Lev. 2:13

349 Not to omit the salt from sacrifices Lev. 2:13

Laws of Sacrificial Procedure

350 Carry out the procedure of the burnt offering as prescribed in the Torah Lev. 1:3

351 Not to eat its meat Deut. 12:17

352 Carry out the procedure of the sin offering Lev. 6:18

353 Not to eat the meat of the inner sin offering Lev. 6:23

354 Not to decapitate a fowl brought as a sin offering Lev. 5:8

355 Carry out the procedure of the guilt offering Lev. 7:1

356 The Kohanim must eat the sacrificial meat in the Temple Ex. 29:33

357 The Kohanim must not eat the meat outside the Temple courtyard Deut. 12:17

358 A non-Kohen must not eat sacrificial meat Ex. 29:33

359 To follow the procedure of the peace offering Lev. 7:11

360 Not to eat the meat of minor sacrifices before sprinkling the blood Deut. 12:17

361 To bring meal offerings as prescribed in the Torah Lev. 2:1

362 Not to put oil on the meal offerings of wrongdoers Lev. 5:11

363 Not to put frankincense on the meal offerings of wrongdoers Lev. 3:11

364 Not to eat the meal offering of the High Priest Lev. 6:16

365 Not to bake a meal offering as leavened bread Lev. 6:10

366 The Kohanim must eat the remains of the meal offerings Lev. 6:9

367 To bring all avowed and freewill offerings to the Temple on the first subsequent festival Deut. 12:5-6

368 Not to withhold payment incurred by any vow Deut. 23:22

369 To offer all sacrifices in the Temple Deut. 12:11

370 To bring all sacrifices from outside Israel to the Temple Deut. 12:26

371 Not to slaughter sacrifices outside the courtyard Lev. 17:4

372 Not to offer any sacrifices outside the courtyard Deut. 12:13

Laws of Constant and Additional Offerings

373 To offer two lambs every day Num. 28:3

374 To light a fire on the altar every day Lev. 6:6

375 Not to extinguish this fire Lev. 6:6

376 To remove the ashes from the altar every day Lev. 6:3

377 To burn incense every day Ex 30:7

378 To light the Menorah every day Ex. 27:21

379 The Kohen Gadol must bring a meal offering every day Lev. 6:13

380 To bring two additional lambs as burnt offerings on Shabbat Num 28:9

381 To make the show bread Ex. 25:30

382 To bring additional offerings on the New Month Num. 28:11

383 To bring additional offerings on Passover Num. 28:19

384 To offer the wave offering from the meal of the new wheat Lev. 23:10

385 Each man must count the Omer - seven weeks from the day the new wheat offering was brought Lev. 23:15

386 To bring additional offerings on Shavuot Num. 28:26

387 To bring two leaves to accompany the above sacrifice Lev. 23:17

388 To bring additional offerings on Rosh Hashana Num. 29:2

389 To bring additional offerings on Yom Kippur Num. 29:8

390 To bring additional offerings on Sukkot Num. 29:13

391 To bring additional offerings on Shmini Atzeret Num. 29:35

Laws of Disqualified Offerings

392 Not to eat sacrifices which have become unfit or blemished Deut. 14.3

393 Not to eat from sacrifices offered with improper intentions Lev. 7:18

394 Not to leave sacrifices past the time allowed for eating them Lev. 22:30

395 Not to eat from that which was left over Lev. 19:8

396 Not to eat from sacrifices which became impure Lev. 7:19

397 An impure person must not eat from sacrifices Lev. 7:20

398 To burn the leftover sacrifices Lev. 7:17

399 To burn all impure sacrifices Lev. 7:19

Law of Yom Kippur Service

400 To follow the procedure of Yom Kippur in the sequence prescribed in Parshat Acharei Mot Lev. 16:3

Laws of Misusing Sanctified Property

401 One who profaned property must repay what he profaned plus a fifth and bring a sacrifice Lev. 5:16

402 Not to work consecrated animals Deut. 15:19

403 Not to shear the fleece of consecrated animals Deut. 15:19

Laws of Pascal Sacrifice

404 To slaughter the paschal sacrifice at the specified time Ex. 12:6

405 Not to slaughter it while in possession of leaven Ex. 23:18

406 Not to leave the fat overnight Ex. 23:18

407 To slaughter the second paschal lamb Num. 9:11

408 To eat the paschal lamb with matzah and Marror on the night of the 15th of Nissan Ex. 12:8

409 To eat the second paschal lamb on the night of the 15th of Iyar Num.9:11

410 Not to eat the paschal meat raw or boiled Ex. 12:9

411 Not to take the paschal meat from the confines of the group Ex. 12:46

412 An apostate must not eat from it Ex.12:43

413 A permanent or temporary hired worker must not eat from it Ex. 12:45

414 An uncircumcised male must not eat from it Ex. 12:48

415 Not to break any bones from the paschal offering Ex. 12:46

416 Not to break any bones from the second paschal offering Num. 9:12

417 Not to leave any meat from the paschal offering over until morning Ex. 12:10

418 Not to leave the second paschal meat over until morning Num. 9:12

419 Not to leave the meat of the holiday offering of the 14th until the 16th Deut. 16:4

Laws of Pilgrim Offerings

420 To be seen at the Temple on Passover, Shavuot, and Sukkot Deut. 16:16

421 To celebrate on these three Festivals (bring a peace offering) Ex. 23:14

422 To rejoice on these three Festivals (bring a peace offering) Deut. 16:14

423 Not to appear at the Temple without offerings Deut. 16:16

424 Not to refrain from rejoicing with, and giving gifts to, the Levites Deut. 12:19

425 To assemble all the people on the Sukkot following the seventh year Deut. 31:12

Laws of First Born Animals

426 To set aside the firstborn animals Ex. 13:12

427 The Kohanim must not eat unblemished firstborn animals outside Jerusalem Deut. 12:17

428 Not to redeem the firstborn Num. 18:17

429 Separate the tithe from animals Lev. 27:32

430 Not to redeem the tithe Lev. 27:33

Laws of Offerings for Unintentional Transgressions

431 Every person must bring a sin offering for his transgression Lev. 4:27

432 Bring an asham talui when uncertain of guilt Lev. 5:17-18

433 Bring an asham vadai when guilt is ascertained Lev. 5:25

434 Bring an oleh v'yored offering (if the person is wealthy, an animal; if poor, a bird or meal offering) Lev. 5:7-11

435 The Sanhedrin must bring an offering when it rules in error Lev. 4:13

Laws of Lacking Atonement

436 A woman who had a running issue must bring an offering after she goes to the Mikveh Lev. 15:28-29

437 A woman who gave birth must bring an offering after she goes to the Mikveh Lev. 12:6

438 A man who had a running issue must bring an offering after he goes to the Mikveh Lev. 15:13-14

439 A metzora must bring an offering after going to the Mikveh Lev. 14:10

Laws of Substitution of Sacrifices

440 Not to substitute another beast for one set apart for sacrifice Lev. 27:10

441 The new animal, in addition to the substituted one, retains consecration Lev. 27:10

442 Not to change consecrated animals from one type of offering to another Lev. 27:26

Law of Impurity of Human Dead

443 Carry out the laws of impurity of the dead Num. 19:14

Laws of The Red Heifer

444 Carry out the procedure of the Red Heifer Num. 19:2

445 Carry out the laws of the sprinkling water Num. 19:21

Laws of Impurity through Tzara'at

446 Rule the laws of human tzara'at as prescribed in the Torah Lev. 13:12

447 The metzora must not remove his signs of impurity Deut. 24:8

448 The metzora must not shave signs of impurity in his hair Lev. 13:33

449 The metzora must publicize his condition by tearing his garments, allowing his hair to grow and covering his lips Lev. 13:45

450 Carry out the prescribed rules for purifying the metzora Lev. 14:2

451 The metzora must shave off all his hair prior to purification Lev. 14:9

452 Carry out the laws of tzara'at of clothing Lev. 13:47

453 Carry out the laws of tzara'at of houses Lev. 13:34

Laws of Impurity of Reclining and Sitting

454 Observe the laws of menstrual impurity Lev. 15:19

455 Observe the laws of impurity caused by childbirth Lev. 12:2

456 Observe the laws of impurity caused by a woman's running issue Lev. 15:25

457 Observe the laws of impurity caused by a man's running issue Lev. 15:3

Laws of Other Sources of Impurity

458 Observe the laws of impurity caused by a dead beast Lev. 11:39

459 Observe the laws of impurity caused by the eight shratzim Lev. 11:29

460 Observe the laws of impurity of a seminal emission Lev. 15:16

Laws of Impurity of Food

461 Observe the laws of impurity concerning liquid and solid foods Lev. 11:34

Laws of Mikveh

462 Every impure person must immerse himself in a Mikveh to become pure Lev. 15:16

Laws of Property Damage

463 The court must judge the damages incurred by a goring ox Ex. 21:28

464 The court must judge the damages incurred by an animal eating Ex. 22:4

465 The court must judge the damages incurred by a pit Ex. 21:33

466 The court must judge the damages incurred by fire Ex. 22:5

Laws of Theft

467 Not to steal money stealthily Lev. 19:11

468 The court must implement punitive measures against the thief Ex. 21:37

469 Each individual must ensure that his scales and weights are accurate Lev. 19:36

470 Not to commit injustice with scales and weights Lev. 19:35

471 Not to possess inaccurate scales and weights even if they are not for use Deut. 25:13

472 Not to move a boundary marker to steal someone's property Deut. 19:14

473 Not to kidnap Ex. 20:13

Laws of Robbery and Lost Objects

474 Not to rob openly Lev. 19:13

475 Not to withhold wages or fail to repay a debt Lev. 19:13

476 Not to covet and scheme to acquire another's possession Ex. 20:14

477 Not to desire another's possession Deut. 5:18

478 Return the robbed object or its value Lev. 5:23

479 Not to ignore a lost object Deut. 22:3

480 Return the lost object Deut. 22:1

481 The court must implement laws against the one who assaults another or damages another's property Ex. 21:18

Laws of Murder and Preservation of Life

482 Not to murder Ex. 20:13

483 Not to accept monetary restitution to atone for the murderer Num. 35:31

484 The court must send the accidental murderer to a city of refuge Num. 35:25

485 Not to accept monetary restitution instead of being sent to a city of refuge Num. 35:32

486 Not to kill the murderer before he stands trial Num. 35:12

487 Save someone being pursued even by taking the life of the pursuer Deut. 25112

488 Not to pity the pursuer Num. 35:12

489 Not to stand idly by if someone's life is in danger Lev. 19:16

490 Designate cities of refuge and prepare routes of access Deut. 19:3

491 Break the neck of a calf by the river valley following an unsolved murder Deut. 21:4

492 Not to work nor plant that river valley Deut. 21:4

493 Not to allow pitfalls and obstacles to remain on your property Deut. 22:8

494 Make a guard rail around flat roofs Deut. 22:8

495 Not to put a stumbling block before a blind man (nor give harmful advice) Lev. 19:14

496 Help another remove the load from a beast which can no longer carry it Ex. 23:5

497 Help others load their beast Deut. 22:4

498 Not to leave others distraught with their burdens (but to help either load or unload) Deut. 22:4

Laws of Sales

499 Buy and sell according to Torah law Lev. 25:14

500 Not to overcharge or underpay for an article Lev. 25:14

501 Not to insult or harm anybody with words Lev. 25:17

502 Not to cheat a sincere convert monetarily Ex. 22:20

503 Not to insult or harm a sincere convert with words Ex. 22:20

Laws of Slaves

504 Purchase a Hebrew slave in accordance with the prescribed laws Ex. 21:2

505 Not to sell him as a slave is sold Lev. 25:42

506 Not to work him oppressively Lev. 25:43

507 Not to allow a non-Jew to work him oppressively Lev. 25:53

508 Not to have him do menial slave labor Lev. 25:39

509 Give him gifts when he goes free Deut. 15:14

510 Not to send him away empty-handed Deut. 15:13

511 Redeem Jewish maidservants Ex. 21:8

512 Betroth the Jewish maidservant Ex. 21:8

513 The master must not sell his maidservant Ex. 21:8

514 Canaanite slaves must work forever unless injured in one of their limbs Lev. 25:46

515 Not to extradite a slave who fled to Israel Deut. 23:16

516 Not to wrong a slave who has come to Israel for refuge Deut. 23:16

Laws of Hiring

517 The courts must carry out the laws of a hired worker and hired guard Ex. 22:9

518 Pay wages on the day they were earned Deut. 24:15

519 Not to delay payment of wages past the agreed time Lev. 19:13

520 The hired worker may eat from the unharvested crops where he works Deut. 23:25

521 The worker must not eat while on hired time Deut. 23:26

522 The worker must not take more than he can eat Deut. 23:25

523 Not to muzzle an ox while plowing Deut. 25:4

Laws of Borrowing and Depositing

524 The courts must carry out the laws of a borrower Ex. 22:13

525 The courts must carry out the laws of an unpaid guard Ex. 22:6

Laws of Creditor and Debtor

526 Lend to the poor and destitute Ex. 22:24

527 Not to press them for payment if you know they don't have it Ex. 22:24

528 Press the idolater for payment Deut. 15:3

529 The creditor must not forcibly take collateral Deut. 24:10

530 Return the collateral to the debtor when needed Deut. 24:13

531 Not to delay its return when needed Deut. 24:12

532 Not to demand collateral from a widow Deut. 24:17

533 Not to demand as collateral utensils needed for preparing food Deut. 24:6

534 Not to lend with interest Lev.25:37

535 Not to borrow with interest Deut. 23:20

536 Not to intermediate in an interest loan, guarantee, witness, or write the promissory note Ex. 22:24

537 Lend to and borrow from idolaters with interest Deut. 23:21

Law of Plaintiff and Defendant

538 The courts must carry out the laws of the plaintiff, admitter, or denier Ex. 22:8

Law of Inheritance

539 Carry out the laws of the order of inheritance Num. 27:8

Laws of Sanhedrin and Punishments

540 Appoint judges Deut. 16:18

541 Not to appoint judges who are not familiar with judicial procedure Deut. 1:17

542 Decide by majority in case of disagreement Ex. 23:2

543 The court must not execute through a majority of one; at least a majority of two is required Ex. 23:2

544 A judge who presented an acquittal plea must not present an argument for conviction in capital cases Deut. 23:2

545 The courts must carry out the death penalty of stoning Deut. 22:24

546 The courts must carry out the death penalty of burning Lev. 20:14

547 The courts must carry out the death penalty of the sword Ex. 21:20

548 The courts must carry out the death penalty of strangulation Lev. 20:10

549 The courts must hang those stoned for blasphemy or idolatry Deut. 21:22

550 Bury the executed on the day they are killed Deut.21:23

551 Not to delay burial overnight Deut. 21:23

552 The court must not let the sorcerer live Ex. 22:17

553 The court must give lashes to the wrongdoer Ex. 25:2

554 The court must not exceed the prescribed number of lashes Deut. 25:3

555 The court must not kill anybody on circumstantial evidence Ex. 23:7

556 The court must not punish anybody who was forced to do a crime Deut. 22:26

557 A judge must not pity the murderer or assaulter at the trial Deut. 19:13

558 A judge must not have mercy on the poor man at the trial Lev. 19:15

559 A judge must not respect the great man at the trial Lev. 19:15

560 A judge must not decide unjustly the case of the habitual transgressor Ex. 23;6

561 A judge must not pervert justice Lev. 19:15

562 A judge must not pervert a case involving a convert or orphan Deut. 24:17

563 Judge righteously Lev. 19:15

564 The judge must not fear a violent man in judgment Deut. 1:17

565 Judges must not accept bribes Ex. 23:8

566 Judges must not accept testimony unless both parties are present Ex. 23:1

567 Not to curse judges Ex. 22:27

568 Not to curse the head of state or leader of the Sanhedrin Ex. 22:27

569 Not to curse any upstanding Jew Lev. 19:14

Laws of Evidence

570 Anybody who knows evidence must testify in court Lev. 5:1

571 Carefully interrogate the witness Deut. 13:15

572 A witness must not serve as a judge in capital crimes Deut. 19:17

573 Not to accept testimony from a lone witness Deut. 19:15

574 Transgressors must not testify Ex. 23:1

575 Relatives of the litigants must not testify Deut. 24:16

576 Not to testify falsely Ex. 20:13

577 Punish the false witnesses as they tried to punish the defendant Deut. 19:19

Laws of Insurgents

578 Act according to the ruling of the Sanhedrin Deut. 17:11

579 Not to deviate from the word of the Sanhedrin Deut. 17:11

580 Not to add to the Torah commandments or their oral explanations Deut. 13:1

581 Not to diminish from the Torah any commandments, in whole or in part Deut. 13:1

582 Not to curse your father and mother Ex. 21:17

583 Not to strike your father and mother Ex. 21:15

584 Respect your father or mother Ex. 20:12

585 Fear your father or mother Lev. 19:3

586 Not to be a rebellious son Deut. 21:18

Laws of Mourning

587 Mourn for relatives Lev. 10:19

588 The High Priest must not defile himself for any relative Lev. 21:11

589 The High Priest must not enter under the same roof as a corpse Lev. 21:11

590 A Kohen must not defile himself for anyone except relatives Lev. 21:1

Laws of Kings and their Wars

591 Appoint a king from Israel Deut. 17:15

592 Not to appoint a convert Deut. 17:15

593 The king must not have too many wives Deut. 17:17

594 The king must not have too many horses Deut. 17:16

595 The king must not have too much silver and gold Deut. 17:17

596 Destroy the seven Canaanite nations Deut. 20:17

597 Not to let any of them remain alive Deut. 20:16

598 Wipe out the descendants of Amalek Deut. 25:19

599 Remember what Amalek did to the Jewish people Deut. 25:17

600 Not to forget Amalek's atrocities and ambush on our journey from Egypt in the desert Deut. 25:19

601 Not to dwell permanently in Egypt Deut. 17:16

602 Offer peace terms to the inhabitants of a city while holding siege, and treat them according to the Torah if they accept the terms Deut. 20:10

603 Not to offer peace to Ammon and Moab while besieging them Deut. 23:7

604 Not to destroy fruit trees even during the siege Deut. 20:19

605 Prepare latrines outside the camps Deut. 23:13

606 Prepare a shovel for each soldier to dig with Deut. 23:14

607 Appoint a priest to speak with the soldiers during the war Deut. 20:2

608 He who has taken a wife, built a new home, or planted a vineyard is given a year to rejoice with his possessions Deut. 24:5

609 Not to demand from the above any involvement, communal or military Deut. 24:5

610 Not to panic and retreat during battle Deut. 20:3

611 Keep the laws of the captive woman Deut. 21:11

612 Not to sell her into slavery Deut. 21:14

613 Not to retain her for servitude after having relations with her Deut. 21:14

There have been many attempts to codify and enumerate the commandments in the Torah. This is a popular version.

The law: An exercise in failure to prove we need Jesus.

The Jews couldn't keep all these laws. So they had a Sin Offering to put them back in right standing with God. The Sin Offering was a perfect lamb to which the sin was transferred on behalf of the sinner, and then the lamb was sacrificed. When sacrificed, the lamb died for the sins of the sinner and the sinner was then without sin.

This whole routine was God's rehearsal, a pantomime, to explain to the Jews the role Jesus was to play in their lives in the future. And God had rehearsed the Jews for generations so they would all understand it when Jesus came.

In the time of the Old Testament and the law, God told mankind, through his prophets, that Jesus was coming and the covenant based on the law would be replaced:

Jeremiah 31:31-34 (KJV)

Behold, **the days are coming, says the Lord, when I will make a new covenant** with the house of Israel and with the house of Judah – not according to the covenant that I made with their fathers in the day that I took them by the hand to lead them out of the land of Egypt, My covenant which they broke, though I was a husband to them, says the Lord. But this is the covenant that I will make with the house of Israel after those days, says the Lord: I will put My law in their minds, and write it on their hearts; and I will be their God, and they shall be My people. No more shall every man teach his neighbor, and every man his brother, saying, "Know the Lord," for they all shall know Me, from the least of them to the greatest of them, says the Lord. **For I will forgive their iniquity, and their sin I will remember no more.**

Jeremiah 50:20 (KJV)

In those days, and in that time, says the LORD, the iniquity of Israel shall be sought for, and there shall be none; **and the sins of Judah, and they shall not be found: for I will pardon them whom I reserve.**

Isaiah 43:25 (KJV)

I, even I, am he that blots out your transgressions for my own sake, and will not remember your sins.

Micah 7:18-19 (KJV)

Who is a God like unto thee, that pardoneth iniquity, and passeth by the transgression of the remnant of his heritage? he retaineth not his anger forever, because he delighteth in mercy. **He will turn again, he will have compassion upon us; he will subdue our iniquities; and thou wilt cast all their sins into the depths of the sea.**

The Old Testament prophets saw the end of the Law of Sin and Death and proclaimed the promise of God's future New Covenant of grace and forgiveness.

God's promises always trump God's "laws". The Laws of Moses did not supersede the promises of God to Abraham that Jesus was coming to those who believe (Galatians 3:15-22). The law was a curse and all who believe on Jesus are all redeemed from this curse.

> Galatians 3:10-14 (NRSV)
>
> **For all who rely on the works of the law are under a curse**: for it is written, "Cursed is everyone who does not observe and obey all the things written in the book of the law." Now it is evident that **no one is justified before God by the law**: for "The one who is righteous will live by faith." But the law does not rest on faith; on the contrary, "Whoever does the works of the law will live by them." **Christ redeemed us from the curse of the law** by becoming a curse for us – for it is written, "Cursed is everyone who hangs on a tree" – in order that in Christ Jesus the blessing of Abraham might come to the Gentiles, so that we might receive the promise of the Spirit through faith.

> Acts 13:38-39 (NRSV)
>
> Let it be known to you therefore, my brothers, that through this man forgiveness of sins is proclaimed to you; **by this Jesus everyone who believes is set free from all those sins for which you could not be freed by the law of Moses.**

So we take the Bible as a whole and see the beautiful story of the law as an important object lesson for mankind.

> Romans 7:4 (NRSV)
>
> In the same way, my friends, you **have died to the law through the body of Christ**, so that you may belong to another, to him who has been raised from the dead in order that we may bear fruit for God.

> John 10:35 (KJV)
>
> If he called them gods, unto whom the word of God came, and **the scripture cannot be broken**;

The law was for a time and for a reason to show us why we must lay down the law in order to embrace what Jesus has died to give us. The law was created so we could learn the failure of the law to save us and why we needed Jesus to step up and finish it for us.

> Matthew 5:17-18 (NKJV)
>
> "Do not think that I have come to destroy the Law or the Prophets. **I did not come to destroy but to fulfill.** For assuredly, I say to you, till heaven and earth pass away, one jot or one tittle will by no means pass from the Law till all is fulfilled."

> Romans 10:1-4 (NKJV)
>
> Brethren, my heart's desire and prayer to God for Israel is that they may be saved. For I bear them witness that they have a zeal for God, but not according to knowledge. **For being ignorant of God's righteousness, and seeking to establish their own righteousness, have not submitted to the righteousness of God. For Christ is the end of the Law for righteousness to everyone who believes.**

Because of Jesus' sacrifice, there is now no law. No law! Our only law is the Law of Life—to believe on the name of Jesus and to love one another.

> Romans 8: 1-2 (NKJV)
>
> There is therefore now no condemnation to those who are in Christ Jesus, who do not walk according to the flesh, but according to the Spirit. **For the law of the Spirit of life in Christ Jesus has made me free from the law of sin and death.**

> Romans 4:13-15 (NRSV)
>
> For the promise that he would inherit the world did not come to Abraham or to his descendants through the law but through the righteousness of faith. If it is the adherence of the law who are to be the heirs, faith is null and the promise

is void. For the law brings wrath; **but where there is no law, neither is there violation.**

Galatians 5:2-6 (NRSV)

Listen! I, Paul, and tell you that if you let yourself be circumcised, Christ will be of no benefit to you. Once again I testify to every man who lets himself be circumcised that he is obliged to obey the entire law. **You who want to be justified by the law have cut yourself off from Christ**: you have fallen away from grace. For through the Spirit, by faith, we eagerly wait for the hope of righteousness. For in Christ Jesus neither circumcision nor uncircumcision counts for anything; the only thing that counts is faith working through love.

Romans 13:8 (KJV)

Owe no man any thing, but to love one another: for **he that loveth another hath fulfilled the law.**

God has changed the covenant.

God has finished his old covenant with us and has made a new covenant with us. Why? Because it is a better covenant.

Hebrews 8:7 (NRSV)

For if that first covenant had been faultless, there would have been no need to look for a second one.

John 1:17 (NKJV)

For the law was given through Moses, **but grace and truth came through Christ Jesus.**

2 Corinthians 3:6 (NKJV)

For the letter killeth, but the Spirit giveth life.

So now that we have no law, what guides us? Through Christ Jesus' sacrifice we have the Holy Spirit within us as our constant advocate, guide, and comforter.

John 14:26 (AMP)

But the Helper (Comforter, Advocate, Intercessor—Counselor, Strengthener, Standby), the Holy Spirit, whom the Father will send in My name [in My place, to represent Me and act on My behalf], He will teach you all things. And He will help you remember everything that I have told you.

Are there any anti-gay laws in the Bible?

No. In the culture of the ancient world, what some have **chosen** to read as *gay*, was a condemnation of straight men of ancient times dominating other straight men through sexual aggression in these two verses from the Old Testament:

Leviticus 18:22 (KJV)

Thou shalt not lie with mankind, as with womankind: it is abomination.

Leviticus 20:13 (KJV)

If a man also lie with mankind, as he lieth with a woman, both of them have committed an abomination: they shall surely be put to death; their blood shall be upon them.

In the Old Testament, straight men were called *men* in the Bible and gay men were called *eunuchs* or (Born Eunuchs by Jesus).

But there are plenty of other laws. There are 28 dietary laws, 13 laws regulating slavery, and 30 laws about court conduct. Are you keeping Kosher? No? Well, don't worry because, according to the Bible, no one is going to Hell for violating any of these laws. The Bible has made the point that the law is an example of how Man would rule the Earth with punishments along the line of an eye-for-an-eye and death for almost any infraction. If scriptural law was honored today we would be a society of blind, toothless (and dead) citizens. Praise God, we are free from the Law of Sin and Death.

This is not a recent revelation. The scriptures warn about religious fervor that creates a ceaseless stream of rules that are not from God:

1 Timothy 4:1-7 (NRSV)

Now the Spirit expressly says that in later times some will renounce the faith by paying attention to deceitful spirits and teachings of demons, through their hypocrisy of liars whose consciences are seared with a hot iron. **They forbid marriage and demand abstinence from foods, which God created to be received with thanksgiving by those who believe and know the truth. For everything created by God is good, and nothing is to be rejected, provided it is received with thanksgiving; for it is sanctified by God's word and by prayer.** If you put these instructions before the brothers and sisters, you will be a good servant of Jesus Christ, nourished on the words of the faith and of the sound teaching that you have followed. Have nothing to do with profane myths and old wives tales. Train yourself in godliness.

Hebrews 13:9 (NRSV)

Do not be carried away by all kinds of strange teachings; for it is well for the heart to be strengthened by grace, not by regulations about food, which has not benefited those who serve them.

Titus 3:8-11 (NRSV)

I desire that you insist on these things, so that those who have come to believe in God may be careful to devote themselves to good works; these things are excellent and profitable to everyone. **But avoid stupid controversies, genealogies, dissensions, and quarrels about the law, for they are unprofitable and worthless.** After a first and second admonition, have nothing more to do with anyone who causes divisions, since you know that such a person is perverted and sinful, being self-condemned.

Through Jesus Christ we are back in the Garden of Eden with only one law, which is not to keep the law.

Do you recall what was that first and only rule given to Adam and Eve?

Genesis 2:17 (NRSV)

"**But from the tree of the knowledge of good and evil you shall not eat**, for in the day that you eat from it you will surely die."

The "Knowledge of Good and Evil" is a description of the law. Man's sin was to know good and evil, to know the law and to judge all things either as good or as evil. We human beings were never designed for the law. We can't keep it and it derails our spiritual life. But now, through Jesus, we are all free from it and back in the same place we were when we were in the Garden.

John 8:32 (NRSV)

"and you will know the truth, and the truth will make you free."

In the Garden there were TWO trees in the center—the Tree of Life and the Tree of the Knowledge of Good and Evil. Our choice—then as now—is to choose the Tree of Life (Jesus) and not eat of the Tree of the Knowledge of Good and Evil (the law). There in the Beginning were the two trees, Jesus and the law. And later, through John, Jesus was revealed as the Tree of Life:

Revelation 2:7 (KJV)

He that hath an ear, let him hear what the Spirit saith unto the churches; To him that overcometh will I give to eat of **the tree of life**, which is in the midst of the paradise of God.

Revelation 22:14 (KJV)

Blessed [are] they that do his commandments, that they may have right to **the tree of life**, and may enter in through the gates into the city.

So we are to choose between Jesus and the law because we cannot have both. When one eats of the law, one is unable to also eat of the Tree of Life, Jesus.

Genesis 3:22-24 (KJV)

And the LORD God said, Behold, the man is become as one of us, to know good and evil: and now, lest he put forth his hand, and take also of the tree of life, and eat, and live for ever: Therefore the LORD God sent him forth from the garden of Eden, to till the ground from whence he was taken. So he drove out the man; and he placed at the east of the garden of Eden Cherubims, and a flaming sword which turned every way, **to keep the way of the tree of life**.

In the Origin Story, Adam and Eve are driven out of the Garden to prevent them from eating of the Tree of Life since they have already eaten of the Tree of the Law, because the two Trees are in conflict — one is Death (the Law of Sin and Death) and the other is Life (Christ Jesus).

Jesus and God are One so this is the choice today between the law and God. Choose God.

John 1:1 (KJV)

In the beginning was the **Word** [Jesus], and the Word was with God, and the **Word was God**.

John 1:14 (NIV)

The Word became flesh and made his dwelling among us. We have seen his glory of the one and only Son, who came from the Father, full of grace and truth.

John 5:39 (KJV)

Search the **scriptures** [The Word]; for in them ye think ye have eternal life: and they are they which testify of **me** [Jesus].

John 10:30 (KJV)

I [Jesus] **and** [my] **Father are one**.

We are now free to NOT eat the wrong fruit.

We are to keep our eyes on Jesus and not be led astray by

-cultural bigotry or
-political fashion or
-tradition or
-the law.

We have come full circle through the scriptures and we have arrived, seated at the right hand of God in Heavenly places, with Christ Jesus. That means all of us — gay, straight, all.

The last prayer Jesus prayed—after the last supper and just before Jesus was led away by Roman soldiers—was that all believers be ONE.

John 17:18-23 (KJV)

Sanctify them through thy truth: thy word is truth. As thou hast sent me into the world, even so have I also sent them into the world. And for their sakes I sanctify myself, that they also might be sanctified through the truth. Neither pray I for these alone, but for them also which shall believe on me through their word; **That they all may be one**; as thou, Father, art in me, and I in thee, **that they also may be one in us:** that the world may believe that thou hast sent me. And the glory which thou gavest me I have given them; **that they may be one**, even as we are one: I in them, and thou in me, **that they may be made perfect in one**; and that the world may know that thou hast sent me, and hast loved them, as thou hast loved me.

Jesus did not come to Earth as a man to establish a black church or a gay church. But, rather, Jesus came to establish ONE Church where we are all one—Jew, Gentile, gay, straight, black, white.

Church is the plural noun for *Believers*. We are all members of the body of Christ ...

> Ephesians 5:29-30 (NIV)
>
> ...After all, no one ever hated their own body, but they feed and care for their body, just as Christ does the church— **for we are members of his body**...

... and Jesus is the head of this body ...

> Colossians 1:18 (KJV)
>
> **And he is the head of the body, the church**: who is the beginning, the firstborn from the dead; that in all things he might have the preeminence.

... and Jesus' body is the Church.

> Colossians 1:24 (KJV)
>
> Who now rejoice in my sufferings for you, and fill up that which is behind of the afflictions of Christ in my flesh for **his body's sake, which is the church**:

And you, my friend, are just maybe a little part of the toenail on Jesus' left pinky toe.

But you are ONE with the whole body, all of us, gay and straight.

Bonus - Gay Marriage

What God means by marriage—
Proof God is for gay marriage.

God is for positive relationships for all of us. So God is for gay marriage and here's the proof.

But first, I will show you what is **Biblical** marriage, the marriage system that is described in the Bible as the custom in Biblical times. This is a system of plural unions, conducted on the pattern of a sales transaction where the Bridegroom purchases the Bride, where he then is required to take care of all her needs, and where he is sovereign in that relationship.

When we talk about marriage today we mean modern marriage—the cute proposal, the big white dress, registering at *Bed Bath and Beyond* and working out whose employer offers the best healthcare plan.

But that is not Biblical marriage. There is no marriage in the Bible that resembles marriage today.

Let's just start with the basics: Is Biblical marriage one man and one woman? No. In the Old Testament there are marriages with many people participating with wifely obligations and rights. These people could be called wives, or concubines, or maids, or female slaves. However, the obligations of husbands are specific and their rights are always superior to those of the many women in the relationship.

Is Biblical marriage something holy? No. In the New Testament, the understanding given to us by the Apostle Paul was that marriage is a distraction to the Christian walk but may be a necessary evil ("It is better to marry than to burn", etc.). Furthermore, we learn from Jesus that the way many people have been understanding marriage and divorce in the Jewish and Christian traditions has not been God's idea at all.

It is foundational to study Biblical marriage in detail because it is the basis for many churches to condemn gay marriage. The popular claim is that gay marriage is against the concept of marriage that is supported in the Bible. Therefore it is a threshold matter that Biblical marriage be completely understood.

How does a man "take" a wife? Through sex.

Throughout the early Old Testament there is a term "taking wives" wherein the early patriarchs of the Old Testament took a wife and often took **wives**, plural (Matthew 24:37 - 38; Luke 17:26 - 27). In the Bible, the marriage is a celebration of a father giving or selling his daughter to the Bridegroom. Then the Bridegroom becomes married to the Bride when he has sex with her—when he "takes" her. He is not married to her just because of the celebration. As proof, read the story of Jacob and how he got two wives when he really only wanted one (Genesis 29:15 - 30):

The story says Jacob was the Bridegroom and they had a big wedding celebration followed by the wedding night but he woke up in bed with the _sister_ of the girl he _thought_ he had married. If this had happened today—if a groom was drunk and didn't know on his wedding night that he had had sex with one of the bridesmaids instead of his wife—it would have been bad but no one would say he was now married to the bridesmaid.

However, in Biblical times, a man takes a wife through having sex with her. So in the story in Genesis, Jacob got a Bride he didn't want because she was switched in the bedroom. As an apology, her father agreed to give him both daughters for an additional 7 years of servitude.

Jacob agreed to work an additional 7 years to have now the girl he really wanted to marry. So then there was a second wedding the next week where Jacob properly consummated the second marriage.

We have it backwards from Biblical days. Today, traditional churches advise sex after marriage. But in Biblical times, the sex came first and that made the marriage. When any young couple had sex, the man then paid the girl's father 50 shekels and they were married.

Keep wife number one . . .

Deuteronomy 22: 28-29 (NRSV)

If a man meets a virgin who is not engaged, and seizes her and lies with her, and they are caught in the act, the man who lay with her shall give 50 shekels of silver to the young woman's father, and she shall become his wife. Because he violated her **he shall not be permitted to divorce her as long as he lives.**

In the Scriptures it says that, "because he violated her, a virgin, he shall not be permitted to divorce her as long as he lives". The violation does not mean rape; it means that he was her first sexual encounter.

The Bible says a man must keep a virginal woman he has married forever (Deuteronomy 22:13 - 19.)

. . . then add more wives as desired.

Today the most common understanding of marriage is that it is a legal relationship between one man and one woman. But this isn't so in the Bible. In the Bible, bishops have been admonished to have "*only*" one wife and God expected kings to "not take *many* wives." But that didn't stop anyone. In addition the Bible makes it clear that a man had legal sexual access to his wives' maids, and he could also purchase concubines who then had the sexual rights and legal financial support as wives. Also female slaves were property for the sexual use of the master of the house. And everyone's children belonged to the husband.

The terms *wife*, *concubine*, and *maid* are frequently interchanged throughout scriptural text, documenting the loose arrangements that could constitute marriage in Biblical times as related in the story of Jacob and his complex marriage to Rachel, Leah, Bihah, and Zilpah (Genesis 46:1 - 27; Genesis 37:2; Genesis 35:22; Genesis 35:22 - 26; Genesis 32:22; Genesis 30:3 - 13; Genesis 46:1 - 17). Concubines may start out as slaves but, when the relationship turns sexual, the concubine assumes the role of a wife and the master assumes the role of a husband (Judges 19:1 - 4, RSV).

Esau, Jacob's elder brother, had many wives (Genesis 28:6 - 9). King David had at least eight wives and at least ten concubines (piecing together many comments in the scriptures including 2 Samuel 3:2 - 5 and 2 Samuel 5:13 - 15). When Sarai/Sarah could not bear children, she gave her slave-girl to Abraham "as his wife" (Genesis 16:3). After Sarah died, Abraham took another wife and then also had concubines who bore him children (Genesis 22:1 - 6). Rehoboam had eighteen wives and sixty concubines (2 Chronicles 11:21). Abijah had fourteen wives (2 Chronicles 13:21). Gideon had many wives and at least one concubine (Judges 8:30 - 31) who is later referred to as a slave woman (Judges 9:18). Solomon had seven hundred wives and three hundred concubines (1 Kings 11:3).

There was no casual heterosexual sex among the Israelites. If a man had sex with a woman, he was obligated to look after her, support her and her children. He had to pay her family for her if she was a free woman.

This system was understood by all the people in the Bible, for whom and by whom the Bible was written.

The husband

And what is the husband's responsibility? The husband was the head of the household and was responsible for all his wives and children. His legal obligation extended to giving each of his wives a son before he dies, so this son assumes all support obligations to his mother for the rest of her life, seeing to her every need. If the husband dies without having a son with his wife, his responsibility to his wife does not die but is accepted by the husband's brother (even if he is already married). And if that brother refuses or dies, this becomes the responsibility of the next brother (Deuteronomy 25:5 - 10).

Is there divorce in the Old Testament?

Why worry about divorce in a world where you could just always add wives? The Bible documents the many wives of kings, but kings were rich. So the desire to be able to divorce may have been a middle-class concern. For those who wanted to stop the upkeep on their old wives, Moses cooked up the idea of divorce (Deuteronomy 24:1 - 4).

But in the New Testament, Jesus made God's position on divorce clear: No divorce.

> Mark 10: 2-12 (NIV)
>
> Some Pharisees came and tested him by asking, "Is it lawful for a man to divorce his wife?" "What did Moses command you?" he replied. They said, "Moses permitted a man to write a certificate of divorce and send her away." "**It was because**

your hearts were hard that Moses wrote you this law," Jesus replied. "But at the beginning of creation God 'made them male and female. ' For this reason a man will leave his father and mother and be united to his wife, and the two will become one flesh.' So they are no longer two, but one flesh. Therefore what God has joined together, let no one separate." When they were in the house again, the disciples asked Jesus about this. He answered, **"Anyone who divorces his wife and marries another woman commits adultery against her. And if she divorces her husband and marries another man, she commits adultery**."

This simple form of marriage is God's ideal. We know this is so because Jesus said he only says what his Father says and he only does what his Father does (John 5:19; John 8:38; John 12:49). So here Jesus is referring to God's idea of Earthly marriage that was illustrated in the marriage of Adam and Eve — fidelity forever, no matter what—no paperwork, just fidelity. So God's idea of Earthly marriage is based on commitment and sexual union, nothing else.

But when God uses marriage as a symbol, as a model for the ancient Jews to be able to understand their relationship to Jesus, he uses the marriage model ancient people were practicing then: plural arrangements, purchased Brides, and un-ending responsibility by the Bridegroom, even after his death.

> **Biblical marriage between men and women and between God and his people follow the same pattern.**

Earthly marriage has moved from two people in the Garden of Eden—no band playing, no paperwork—to multiple wives and armies of children from complex domestic relations that rips the limits of the term "extended family" and then, in the New Testament, back again to a solitary pair.

But still, this solitary pair was, in those times, created through the customs of the times that included buying the Bride through one form or another (war, barter, livestock). So if you lived in those times, your mother would have been bought from your grandfather and your wife would have been bought for you, and you will buy a wife for your son. Men were married and women were taken in marriage.

**Marriage in the Bible was a covenant,
a serious contract with your family.**

God used the term *marriage* in the Bible because he was speaking to a people who would understand what he was talking about by that term. In the Bible, God is married to all who are believers in him.

> Isaiah 54:5-8 (NIV)
>
> For your Creator will be your **husband**. The LORD Almighty is his name! He is your Redeemer, the Holy One of Israel, the God of all the earth. For the LORD has called you back from your grief — as though you were a **young wife** abandoned by her **husband**," says your God. "For a brief moment I abandoned you, but with great compassion I will take you back. In a moment of anger I turned my face away for a little while. But with everlasting love I will have compassion on you," says the LORD, your Redeemer.

Here God said he will be the husband to you who have no husband or to those whose husband walked out on them. He was not speaking only to women. He was speaking to all people. God used the word *husband* and *marriage* so that the readers in this ancient world would understand what he meant.

God means he will protect you, support you, feed you and be responsible for you. He will take care of your children, clothe you, and defend you. The *you* in this verse is the Bride, the young wife, the most loved wife, the first wife. If you are a man, God says he will protect you and love you and take care of you, his Bride. And God hates divorce so he will never divorce you. God is saying he is married to all men who believe and trust in him, that he, God, will be their husband. So God Himself uses the word *marriage* without any gender identifying the parties in this marriage. In God's idea of marriage there is no gender. In the Bible the term *marriage* is a forever contract of protection and support.

Jesus is the Bridegroom, taking all of us as his Bride.

In the Bible, both God and Jesus take the role of the husband to us all. Jesus is referred to many times in the Bible as the Bridegroom and we are the Bride. This is because the Bible is using scriptural marriage to explain our relationship to Jesus. Just like Brides in Biblical times, Jesus bought us with a price. Jesus, the Bridegroom, paid the price for us on the cross with his blood. These are scriptures that refer to this gathering of the Church — the believers in Christ — to Jesus, as a marriage:

Revelation 19:7-9 (KJ21)

Let us be glad and rejoice, and give honor to him: for the **marriage** of the Lamb is come, and his **wife** hath made herself ready. And to her was granted that she should be arrayed in fine linen, clean and white: for the fine linen is the righteousness of saints. And he saith unto me, "Write, Blessed [are] they which are called unto the **marriage** supper of the Lamb." And he saith unto me, "These are the true sayings of God."

Revelation 21:9 (KJV)

And there came unto me one of the seven angels which had the seven vials full of the seven last plagues, and talked with me, saying, Come hither, I will shew thee the **brid**e, the Lamb's **wife**.

2 Corinthians 11:2 (KJV)

For I am jealous over you with godly jealousy: for I have espoused you to one **husband**, that I may present [you as] a chaste **virgin** to Christ.

Romans 7:4 (KJV)

Wherefore, my brethren, ye also are become dead to the

law by the body of Christ; that ye should be **married** to another, [even] to him who is raised from the dead, that we should bring forth fruit unto God.

And when Jesus dies, he replaces himself with the Holy Spirit who will then step in as our unending support.

John 16:7 (KJV)

Nevertheless I tell you the truth; **It is expedient for you that I go away**: for if I go not away, the Comforter will not come unto you; but **if I depart, I will send him unto you.**

John 14:16 (AMPC)

And I will ask the Father, and He will give you another Comforter (Counselor, Helper, Intercessor, Advocate, Strengthener, and Standby), **that He may remain with you forever —**

In the scriptures, Jesus is the Bridegroom, and we are the Bride. The marriage feast is being prepared. So, in all this, where the Bible speaks so plainly about marriage, there is no reference to sex or to gender as believers in Jesus are both men and women.

In the Bible, God says marriage is the closest relationship one can have with another. And if God can be married to us all—both to men and to women—then marriage, in the eyes of God, is not limited by gender. In the Bible, the marriage is not about gender. It is about relationship. Because God has made this clear, that marriage is about a covenant, not about gender, then God is in favor of marriage for all genders.

Does God want us married?

As we have seen in the scriptures, Jesus is in favor of marriage (Matthew 19:4 - 6). In this world there will be tribulation! (John 16:33). In this world we will need a husband to protect us. Our marriages are in this world with the tribulation.

That is why there is no marriage in Heaven. We don't need it. There is no tribulation in Heaven and there is no sex in Heaven:

> Matthew 22: 23-30 (NIV)
>
> That same day the Sadducees, who say there is no resurrection, came to him with a question. "Teacher," they said, "Moses told us that if a man dies without having children, his brother must marry the widow and raise up offspring for him. Now there were seven brothers among us. The first one married and died, and since he had no children, he left his wife to his brother. The same thing happened to the second and third brother, right on down to the seventh. Finally, the woman died. Now then, at the resurrection, whose wife will she be of the seven, since all of them were married to her?"
>
> Jesus replied, "You are in error because you do not know the Scriptures or the power of God. **At the resurrection people will neither marry nor be given in marriage; they will be like the angels in heaven.** "

Luke reports Jesus' words this way:

> Luke 20: 34-36 (NIV)
>
> Jesus replied, **"The people of this age marry and are given in marriage. But those who are considered worthy of taking part in the age to come and in the resurrection from the dead will neither marry nor be given in marriage, and they can no longer die; for they are like the angels.** They are God's children, since they are children of the resurrection. "

And the apostle Mark quotes Jesus this way:

> Mark 12: 23-25 (NIV)
>
> "At the resurrection whose wife will she be, since the seven were married to her?" Jesus replied, "Are you not in error because you do not know the Scriptures or the power of

God? **When the dead rise, they will neither marry nor be given in marriage; they will be like the angels in heaven. "**

Marriage throughout the Bible stories was a relationship borne out of the sex act. A concubine was elevated to the status of 'wife' through the sex act. A fiancée becomes a wife at the sex act.

There is no sex in Heaven. So there is no marriage in Heaven. But God wants us married on Earth for the many reasons he gave — help and companionship (Genesis 2:18 - 20) and protection from sex outside of a committed relationship ("better to marry than to burn", 1 Corinthians 7:9).

The hope of gay marriage in this world.

The Bible is progressive. It moves from a One Law system to a 613 Law System then to a Two Law System.

It moves from Adam having authority in this world

> Genesis 1:26-28

to Satan having authority in this world

> 2 Corinthians 4:4
>
> John 12:31
>
> John 14:30
>
> Luke 4:5-6

to Christ having authority in this world

> Matthew 11:27
>
> Matthew 28:18
>
> John 3:35
>
> Philippians 2:9
>
> Colossians 2:10

to us having authority in this world through him.

Matthew 10:1

Matthew 16:19

Mark 3:15

Mark 6:7

Mark 16:17-18

Luke 10:19

Psalm 8:4-6

If the Bible wasn't progressive, the Jews would still be in Egypt.

We are continuing on that progressive trajectory today. However the echoes of our not-that-ancient past and our inequality in dealing with the genders still ripples across all heterosexual relationships. Therefore, it is quite possible that gay marriage—the pairing of two men or two women—is the first marriage structure to arrive on the human stage without the historic ghost of gender inequality. God's original desire for Adam and Eve was for them to be equal partners. It was never God's plan that women be in the submissive, subservient role Biblical women lived after the Garden of Eden (Galatians 3:28).

The Bible supports same-sex relationships, sexual or not. In Ecclesiastes, here are passages that are often quoted at weddings although these verses are actually written about a man longing for a male companion:

Ecclesiastes 4:9-12 (NKJV)

Two are better than one, because they have a good reward for their labor. For if they fall, one will lift up his companion. But woe to him who is alone when he falls, for he has no one to help him up. Again, to lie down together, they will keep warm; but how can one be warm alone? Though one may be overpowered by another, two can withstand him. A threefold cord is not quickly broken.

In these prayerful musings, the writer longs for a relationship of equals. This man from Biblical times cannot imagine such a relationship is possible between a man and a woman. So he is speaking of a hoped for relationship with another man that he likens to a son or brother.

> Ecclesiastes 4:8 (NKJV)
>
> There is one alone, without companion: **He has neither son nor brother**. Yet *there is* no end to all his labors, Nor is his eye satisfied with riches. *But he never asks,* "For whom do I toil and deprive myself of good?" This also *is* vanity and a grave misfortune.

A relationship of equals is the goal of us all — gay and straight. And this is what God wants for us all. God wants us doubly married — married to Jesus and married to a partner on this Earth who supports us, helps us, and loves us—gay or straight.

Next Step

**We can fix this because the gay 'issue' in the
Church is manmade, not God-made.**

Most denominational churches are on record representing God as a homo-phobe and that gays and lesbians are mistakes. On the other hand, the "liberal" Christian and New Age-y churches downplay the gay issue and use humanistic arguments to support their inclusion policies, not scripture. And, sadly, the latest Catholic attitude is "tolerance", but not equality in the eyes of God.

As much as I am glad there is a growing number of churches that include the gay congregant, any non-scriptural basis for this stance makes it seem that Christians can support gay Christianity only through their supposedly more highly-refined social conscience, not because it is the Word of God. That sort of unscriptural thinking can lead Christians to distrust their own faith as they cherry-pick among which of life's issues they will permit themselves to be led by the Word of God and which ones they will not because they can't trust the Word of God to always "do the right thing."

One does not have to read the polls to observe a softening of church atten-dance and a downward trend of those who believe they can trust in God in all matters. In the courthouses and on our money it still says "In God We Trust." But if Christian leaders do not support their pro-gay stand with scripture and teach the Word from their pulpits, it will have the effect of moving this country away from a population that trusts in God. Leaning on humanistic philosophies for our moral strength will make it easier for future Americans to possibly remove these precious words, 'In God We Trust,' from our public places and national symbols.

The disconnect—between what denominational churches are professing and what more and more Christians personally believe is Jesus' own pro-gay stance—is weakening the Church. The Church is not a building. It is all of us and we are to be the body of Christ with Jesus as the head. We cannot accept a weakening of the body of Christ.

> 1 Corinthians 1:10 (KJV)
>
> Now I beseech you, brethren, by the name of our Lord Jesus Christ, **that ye all speak the same thing, and that there be no divisions among you**; but that ye be perfectly joined together in the same mind and in the same judgment.

Why would a minister not publicly teach that God made us all, loves us all, and wants to save us all?

The current anti-gay bias is what the Bible calls "tradition", just doing what is usually done. But the Bible says that choosing tradition (cultural bias) over scripture can cancel the Word of God.

> Mark 7:13 (NLT)
>
> And so **you cancel the word of God in order to hand down your own tradition**. And this is only one example among many others.

Just as the Jewish religious leaders in the time of Jesus were unable to accept what the Word of God actually said but, rather, would cling to their traditional religious ways, many of our church leaders today are the current Pharisees, clinging to a church's religious traditions rather than to seek the truth from the Word itself. Just as it was in the time of Jesus, with religious leaders afraid to attract criticism from their peers, some of today's Christian denominations have painted themselves into a corner through endlessly repeating unscriptural, un-Godly, anti-gay statements. They may believe themselves to be in a tough position with congregations and church authorities if they change their tune now.

We can fix it!

You are not a preacher. But you are a Christian. You are a follower of Jesus. You can help fix this anti-gay bias by communicating to your church leadership that they will not be kicked out for being in line with the written Word of God.

All ministers—especially the most public ones—are afraid of being kicked out of the "Christian Club." To keep to the anti-gay line is the safe road for them. Yes, they might possibly receive some criticism for a homophobic comment phrased indelicately, but to most preachers, that is preferable to being shut out of their entire denomination by preaching that God made gay and it is no mistake.

What is the hope for these ministers? As their more scriptural and Christ-centered congregants depart, their church becomes more entrenched in this crippling anti-gay rhetoric.

This is what I can do. I am sowing this book into churches and organizations and anyone with an Internet connection. I believe that God will supernaturally place this book into the hearts and hands of ministers and congregants. I believe that this scriptural pro-gay understanding will soon become mainstream Christian thought and the era of Christian gay-bashing will quickly become a distant memory right up there with women keeping silent in church.

I believe that Christians everywhere will see themselves as followers of Jesus Christ and not as any specific denomination. I believe that Christians will decide to only do what Jesus does and only say what Jesus says.

I ask you to also sow this book into your church and Bible Study groups. I am convinced that when one sees the revelations of how the gay issue has been twisted and when one sees the real message of the Bible in regards to this issue, the more we will see this truth coming through every Bible sermon, out of every preacher's mouth, whether or not that preacher intended to teach this message or not.

In development – *The Gay Bible*

A new Bible version is now in development. *The Gay Bible* is the full scriptural text that reveals what the original Bible has been saying all along, that:

> -God made us all, gay and straight (John 1:3 *All things were made by him; and without him was not anything made that was made*).
>
> -God loves us all, regardless of our gender or sexual orientation (John 3:16).
>
> -And his expression of himself is through us, his creations (Genesis 1:27).

The Gay Bible more clearly and directly speaks to the gay man or woman to keep the personal connection God intends. *The Gay Bible* makes it clear that God created gay people, God put himself in each gay person, and that God has a plan for every gay person in this world.

Join our http://www.godisgay.com/contact-us/ to be alerted when *The Gay Bible* is released.

Join our community

To Like us on Facebook, go here: https://www.facebook.com/godisgay.thebook/.

Write a review of *God is Gay*

Please write an honest review of this book on the website where you acquired it. It will help me and future readers.

I have written every word of this book through meditation on the Word of God and through what I believe to be Divine Guidance.

I ask that if there is anything in this book that offends you, please prayerfully ask our Maker to speak to your heart and reveal to you the truth of these matters.

Do not take my writings at face value. Only God can lead you to rightly divide the Word for yourself.

I welcome your thoughts and revelations that you may have on this subject.

—C.S. Clement

Published Homosexual References

Current Bibles that use the word *homosexual* are on scholastic thin ice.

Many Bibles have verses where their translators have decided where God *meant* to say *homosexual*, but they cannot agree among themselves where God meant to say it. In these Bible translations, there are as few as a single *homosexual* reference to as many as six *homosexual* references. But they are all wrong.

The oldest Bible translation in common use today is the **Geneva Bible** from 1599. Here are the most popular subsequent later translations by their initial copyright date:

Bibles that do not include the word *homosexual*:

1599	GNV	Geneva Bible
1611	KJV	King James Version
1862	YLT	Young's Literal Translation
1867	DARBY	Darby Translation

1899   DRA   Douay-Rheims American Edition

1901   ASV   American Standard Version

1946   RSV   Revised Standard Version

1960   PHILLIPS J.B. Phillips New Testament

1969   NLV   New Life Version

1969   WE   Worldwide English (New Testament)

1970   NABRE New American Bible Revised Edition

1989   NRSV   New Revised Standard Version

1993   MSG   The Message

1994   KJ21   21st Century King James Version

2001   WYC   Wycliffe Bible

2005   NCV   New Century Version

2011   CEB   Common English Bible

Bibles that include the word *homosexual*:

1954   AMPC   Amplified Bible Classic Edition
        1 Corinthians 6:9

1960   NASB   New American Standard Bible
        1 Corinthians 6:9, 1 Timothy 1:10

1965   RSVCE   Revised Standard Version Catholic Edition
        1 Corinthians 6:9

1969   WEB   World English Bible
        1 Corinthians 6:9, 1 Timothy 1:10

1971 TLB Living Bible
Leviticus 18:22, Leviticus 20:13, Deuteronomy 23:17-18, 1 Kings 14:24, 1 Corinthians 6:9, 1 Timothy 1:10

1973 NIV New International Version
1 Timothy 1:10

1979 NIVUKNew International Version-UK
1 Timothy 1:10

1982 NKJV New King James Version
1 Corinthians 6:9

1992 GNT Good News Translation
1 Corinthians 6:9

1995 CEV Contemporary English Version
1 Corinthians 6:9, 1 Timothy 1:10

1995 GW GOD'S WORD Translation
1 Corinthians 6:9, 1 Timothy 1:10, Jude 1:7

1995 ISV International Standard Version
Judges 19:15, 1 Corinthians 6:9, 1 Timothy 1:10, Jude 1:7

1996 NET New English Translation
1 Corinthians 6:9, 1 Timothy 1:10

1996 NIRV New International Reader's Version
1 Timothy 1:10

1996 NLT New Living Translation
Leviticus 18:22, Leviticus 20:13, 1 Corinthians 6:9, 1 Timothy 1:10

1999 HCSB Holman Christian Standard Bible
1 Corinthians 6:9, 1 Timothy 1:10

2000   JUB   Jubilee Bible 2000
1 Corinthians 6:9, 1 Timothy 1:10

2001   ESV   English Standard Version
1 Corinthians 6:9, 1 Timothy 1:10

2006   ERV   Easy-to-Read Version
1 Timothy 1:10

2011   DLNT   Disciples' Literal New Testament
1 Corinthians 6:9, 1 Timothy 1:10

2011   EXB   Expanded Bible
1 Corinthians 6:9-10, 1 Timothy 1:10

2011   MOUNCE Mounce Reverse-Interlinear New Testament
1 Corinthians 6:9, 1 Timothy 1:10

2011   NOG   Names of God Bible
1 Corinthians 6:9, 1 Timothy 1:10, Jude 1:7

2012   LEB   Lexham English Bible
1 Corinthians 6:9, 1 Timothy 1:10

2012   VOICE The Voice
1 Timothy 1:10

2014   MEV   Modern English Version
1 Corinthians 6:9

2015   AMP   Amplified Bible
1 Corinthians 6:9, 1 Timothy 1:10

These are the verses that have included the word homosexual by major Bible publishers.

1 Corinthians 6:9

The first scripture to be published
using the word homosexual:
1954 Amplified Bible, Classic Edition

In 1954 the editors of the Amplified Bible, Classic Edition, were the first Bible translators to claim 1 Corinthians 6:9 included the word *homosexual*.

Here is the King James Version:

> 1 Corinthians 6:9: **King James Version (1611)**
>
> Know ye not that the unrighteous shall not inherit the kingdom of God? Be not deceived: neither fornicators, nor idolaters, nor adulterers, **nor effeminate, nor abusers of themselves with mankind**,

And here is how this verse was wrongly translated:

> 1 Corinthians 6:9: **Amplified Bible, Classic Edition (1954)**
>
> Do you not know that the unrighteous *and* the wrongdoers will not inherit *or* have any share in the kingdom of God? Do not be deceived (misled): neither the impure *and* immoral, nor idolaters, nor adulterers, **nor those who participate in homosexuality**,

Here the translators of the Amplified Bible have taken the two Greek terms that the King James had translated as *effeminate* (**malakos**) and *abusers of themselves with mankind* (**arsenokoital**)—now thought to refer to the active and the passive participant in the common sexual culture of pederasty as practiced by the merchant classes and ruling classes of ancient Greece—and call this *homosexual activity*.

Did the translators of the Amplified Bible not know of these cultural norms in Ancient Greece in Bible times? [*Dawson, Cities of the Gods, p. 193. See also*

George Boys-Stones, "Eros in Government: Zeno and the Virtuous City," <u>Classical Quarterly</u> 48 (1998), 168–174: "there is a certain kind of sexual relationship which was considered by many Greeks to be very important for the cohesion of the city: sexual relations between men and youths. Such relationships were taken to play such an important role in fostering cohesion where it mattered — among the male population — that Lycurgus even gave them official recognition in his constitution for Sparta" (p. 169).]

Did the translators of the Amplified Bible not know about the systemic sexual culture of penis worship in ancient Greece? [*R. Joy Littlewood, <u>A Commentary on Ovid</u>: Fasti <u>Book 6</u> (Oxford University Press, 2006), p. 73; T.P. Wiseman, <u>Remus: A Roman Myth</u> (Cambridge University Press, 1995), p. 61 online*] [*Joseph Rykwert, <u>The Idea of a Town: The Anthropology of Urban Form in Rome, Italy, and the Ancient World</u> (MIT Press, 1988), pp. 101 and 159*].

Or did the translators of the Amplified Bible believe that somehow the majority of the married male population in Ancient Greece within the merchant and ruling classes were actually gay?

This last supposition is not a reasonable assumption. So, the translators of the Amplified Bible appear to be ignorant of the historical facts that provide material context for this verse. They did not know how these words were used in the time of their authorship.

If Paul wished to call out these men as gay, there certainly were many words in common use in First Century Greece that were used to denote gay men such as *euryproktoi, kinaidos, arrenomanes*, or *pathikos*. But Paul did not use these common words.

Also, in this verse, Paul does not refer to female-on-female sex or lesbianism. Because there is no phallus involved, it is most likely that Paul did not consider this activity between women to be sex. Paul was a Christian, but he was also a man of his time. Sex in ancient Greece was what one *did* to another person and it was *done* with a penis. Sex was always an act of dominance, an expression of a superior social position over another, male or female. In the culture of Ancient Greece, it would not be possible to execute the sex act without the phallus.

Paul did not at any time identify lesbians as sinners although he had the language to do so, if he so desired, as there were many first century Greek words for what we would today call lesbianism: *dihetaristriai, frictrix, hetairstrai, lesbiai, tribades,* or *tribas.*

In 1954, the publishers of the Amplified Bible Classic were the first to corrupt this line of scripture which then opened the door for 20 other published translations to follow suit. The publishers of the Amplified Bible then repeated their original error in their most recent version of their Amplified Bible in 2015, which makes a total of 22 Bible translations of this verse out there, all wrongly reflecting God's heart on this important issue.

1 Timothy 1:10

The second scripture to first be published using the word homosexual: 1960 New American Standard Bible

In 1960 the editors of the New American Standard were the first Bible translators to claim 1 Timothy 1:10 included the word *homosexual.*

Here is the King James Version:

> 1 Timothy 1:10: **King James Version (1611)**
>
> For whoremongers, **for them that defile themselves with mankind,** for menstealers, for liars, for perjured persons, and if there be any other thing that is contrary to sound doctrine;

And here is how this verse was wrongly translated:

> 1 Timothy 1:10: **New American Standard Bible (1960)**

and immoral men and **homosexuals** and kidnappers and liars and perjurers, and whatever else is contrary to sound teaching,

The Greek term translated here by the NASB as *homosexuals* is the same Greek word, **arsenokoiai,** that Paul used in 1 Corinthians 6:9 that many believe refers to the active partner in the male-on-male sex act. In the first verse, Paul was writing to the church in Corinth, Greece. There Paul chose to say that both the straight male active partner and the straight male passive partner who permits the act were to blame for the misconduct.

However, in this verse, 1 Timothy 1:10, Paul only calls out the straight male active partner for chastisement. This letter to Timothy was written approximately 10 years after Paul wrote a similar sentiment in his letter to the Corinthians that contains the verse 1 Corinthians 6:9 previously discussed. So although the two verses—1 Corinthians 6:9 and 1 Timothy 1:10—cover the same subject matter, in 1 Timothy Paul only criticizes the behavior of the straight male active partner in the verse authored last, perhaps later believing the passive straight (probably young) male as being a victim.

Again, if Paul wished to call out these men as gay, there certainly were many words in common use in First Century Greece that were used to denote gay men such as *euryproktoi, kinaidos, arrenomanes,* or *pathikos.* But Paul did not use these common words.

The other argument against this Greek term **arsenokoiai** in this verse as representing a gay man is the same argument that was made in the 1 Corinthians 6:9 discussion—that this male-on-male sexual conduct of the day was so common that it would render a very large percentage of the Greek male population to be gay, a much larger percentage than it is reasonable to consider possible.

Also, again Paul does not include sexual contact between women here as an issue although there were many commonly used first century Greek words for this sexual female behavior such as *dihetaristriai, frictrix, hetairstrai, lesbiai, tribades,* or *tribas.* So, the issue of same-sex partners is not Paul's issue.

After 1 Timothy 1:10 had been corrupted in the New American Standard Bible (NASB) in 1960, twenty other Bible publishers later repeated this error.

It is interesting to note that although 1 Corinthians 6:9 and 1 Timothy 1:10 both share the same number of erroneous Bible translations, twenty-one, the list of publishers making this choice in their translations of the two verses is not the same list although the Greek word **arsenokoitai** is the same term at issue in both scriptures. This begs the question; on what academic basis did these translators interpret the same Greek word so differently from each other and interpret the same Greek word differently within the same translation?

Leviticus 18:22
Leviticus 20:13
Deuteronomy 23:17 – 18
1 Kings 14:24

The third, fourth, fifth, and sixth

scriptures to first be published

using the word homosexual:

1971 The Living Bible translation

In 1971 editors of The Living Bible were the first translators to interpret the above four verses as scriptures that should include the word *homosexual.*

The first two scriptures, Leviticus 18:22 and Leviticus 20:13, are similar.

Here is the King James Version of the first verse:

Leviticus 18:22: **King James Version (1611)**

Thou shalt not lie with mankind, as with womankind: it is abomination.

And here is how this verse was wrongly translated:

Leviticus 18:22: **The Living Bible (1971)**

Homosexuality is absolutely forbidden, for it is an enormous sin.

Here is the King James Version of the second verse:

Leviticus 20:13: **King James Version (1611)**

If a man also lie with mankind, as he lieth with a woman, both of them have committed an abomination: they shall surely be put to death; their blood shall be upon them.

And here is how this verse was wrongly translated:

Leviticus 20:13: **The Living Bible (1971)**

The penalty for **homosexual acts** is death to both parties. They have brought it upon themselves.

These two verses are from the Old Testament and were originally written in Ancient Hebrew. In both these verses, the Hebrew language of the Old Testament refers to the sin of a man having sexual relations with a man as he would a woman. However, in the Hebrew Old Testament, gay men were never referred to as men—not ever. A gay man was a *eunuch*, and a straight man was a *man*. [*"Wells, Collin. Review of The Perfect Servant: Eunuchs and the Social Construction of Gender in Byzantium, 2003 by Kathryn M. Ringrose". Retrieved 2006-10-21*]; [*"Review of Herdt, Gilbert (ed.) (1994) Third Sex, Third Gender: Beyond Sexual Dimorphism in Culture and History". Retrieved 2006-10-21.*] These verses refer to straight men having sex with straight men. This is made all the more obvious as, in both verses, the man in question is assumed to also have sex with women.

This is the first time these two scriptures—Leviticus 18:22 and Leviticus 20:3—have been erroneously translated to include the word *homosexual*. This distortion of these two scriptures has since been repeated once more, by the translators of the New Living Translation (NLT) in 1996.

In the same Living Bible translation of 1971, the authors added the word *homo-sexual*, for the first time, to two additional verses, Deuteronomy 23:17 - 18 and 1 Kings 14:24.

These two verses are from the Old Testament and were originally written in Ancient Hebrew.

Here is the King James Version of the first verse:

Deuteronomy 23:17-18: **King James Version (1611)**

There shall be no whore of the daughters of Israel, **nor a sod-omite** of the sons of Israel.

Thou shalt not bring the hire of a whore, **or the price of a dog**, into the house of the LORD thy God for any vow: for even both these are abomination unto the LORD thy God.

And here is how this verse was wrongly translated:

Deuteronomy 23:17-18: **The Living Bible (1971)**

No prostitutes are permitted in Israel, either men or women; you must not bring to the Lord any offering from the earnings of a prostitute **or a homosexual**, for both are detestable to the Lord your God.

Here is the King James Version of the second verse:

1 Kings 14:24: **King James Version (1611)**

And there were also **sodomites in the land**: and they did according to all the abominations of the nations which the LORD cast out before the children of Israel.

And here is how this verse was wrongly translated:

1 Kings 14:24: **The Living Bible (1971)**

> There was **homosexuality throughout the land**, and the peo-
> ple of Judah became as depraved as the heathen nations
> which the Lord drove out to make room for his people.

In both these verses, the translators of The Living Bible interpreted the word *sodomite* as *homosexual*. However, through reading the correct King James Version of the verses, it is clear the Biblical author was referring to temple prostitutes as the word *sodomite* has consistently been understood to always mean *male temple prostitutes*. The Deuteronomy verse calls the male offender *the price of a dog* which can only refer to someone who is paid for and cannot be referring to a non-prostitute, gay or straight.

In the verse from 1 Kings, the word *sodomite* refers to the paid participant in a sexually extreme pagan religion which was, at that time, a foreign influence in Judah.

By replacing the word *sodomites* with the word *homosexuality*, 1 Kings 14:24 in The Living Bible translation of this verse reads as if same-sex attraction was contagious—it says that there were gay men throughout Judah and therefore the Jews started to turn gay from this gay influence. That makes no sense.

Actually, the scripture refers to the foreign influence of extreme sexual pagan worship which was being adopted by the local Jews of the land. The local Jews were being attracted to the various pagan sex religions and abandoning their Jewish religion.

This is the first and only time these two scriptures—Deuteronomy 23:17 - 18 and 1 Kings 14:24—have been corrupted and misinterpreted to mean *gay*.

Jude 1:7

The seventh scripture to first be published
using the word homosexual:
1995 God's Word translation

In the 1995, the new God's Word translation was published, and it added the word *homosexual* to its translation of Jude 1:7.

Here is the King James Version:

> Jude 1:7: **King James Version (1611)**
>
> Even as Sodom and Gomorrah, and the cities about them in like manner, giving themselves over to fornication, and **going after strange flesh**, are set forth for an example, suffering the vengeance of eternal fire.

And here is how this verse was wrongly translated:

> Jude 1:7: **God's Word (1995)**
>
> What happened to Sodom and Gomorrah and the cities near them is an example for us of the punishment of eternal fire. The people of these cities suffered the same fate that God's people and the angels did, because they committed sexual sins and **engaged in homosexual activities**.

The accurate King James Version states in Jude 7 that the people of Sodom and Gomorrah were *fornicators* which the Bible says is using another for sexual self-gratification and/or abusing others through sex. This *sexual sin* could be on the spectrum from insincere seduction to rape but, since we know the story of Sodom, we know this verse is referring to rape. The God's Word translation of the Bible converts this to *sexual sin* as have many contemporary translations that pre-date their 1995 translation.

Oddly, it is the phrase *going after strange flesh* that has been translated in the new God's Word Bible of 1995 as *engaged in homosexual activities*.

However, in the story of Sodom (Genesis 19) there were no homosexual activities. The mob wanted to abuse the male visitors (the angels), but they did not. They were unable to touch them because the angels blinded them.

In the story of Sodom, the mob banged on Lot's door and demanded that Lot surrender his visitors to them so they could rape them. The mob wanted to attack the angels because they learned the angels were there to destroy the town.

Lot offered the violent mob his own daughters to appease them, which make no sense if the mob is seeking gay sex.

But the mob did not rape the visitors. They never touched the visitors. They banged on the door and yelled and then the angels supernaturally caused the mob members to be struck blind and the threat pretty much ended there. The next day the angels destroyed the towns as planned.

The story actually describes threatening, menacing, harassing, maybe battery (they struck Lot). But nothing that conforms to the translators' published phrase: *engaged in homosexual activities.*

The mob threatened violence. Thankfully, their plans were thwarted. However, even if the mob had succeeded in attacking the visitors, it would not be because they were gay. That would be like claiming all the male rape in prisons today is perpetrated by gay prisoners. I don't think so.

The story of Sodom is about threatening violent sexual humiliation by a group of straight men against strangers to their town.

To translate this as homosexuals seeking sex is a perversion of the word of God.

This is the first time this scripture, Jude 1:7, was corrupted and this error was repeated once more in 2011 by the translators of the Names of God Bible (NOG).

Judges 19:15

The eighth scripture to first be published

using the word *homosexual* :

1995 International Standard Version

In 1995, another translation of the Bible, the International Standard Version, chose to add the word *homosexual* to a place in the scriptures where it had not been previously—Judges 19:15.

Here is the King James Version:

Judges 19:15: **King James Version (1611)**

And they turned aside thither, to go in and to lodge in Gibeah: and when he went in, he sat him down in a street of the city: for there was no man that took them into his house to lodging.

And here is how this verse was wrongly translated:

Judges 19:15: **International Standard Version (1995)**

They turned aside there, intending to enter Gibeah and spend the night.

The Homosexual Descendants of Benjamin in Gibeah

After they entered the city, they had to sit down in the public square because no one would take them into their home for the night.

In the ISV translation, the translators have added large-sized font headings throughout the scriptures as a navigational tool. Here they have inserted such a heading at the beginning of the story of a woman's rape and murder by a violent mob of men and have erroneously (and oddly) identified the men who raped this woman as homosexuals.

The story of Gibeah and the story of Sodom is the same story, just different towns. A violent mob of straight men was going after a visitor to the village. But, in the story of Gilbeah, it is even more obvious what was the violent intent. In the story of Gibeah, the intended victim later witnessed that the mob was endeavoring to inflict a violent attack upon him that would lead to his murder. The man saved himself from death by giving the violent mob his mistress. So, this violent mob raped and murdered her instead.

This does not describe a gay mob.

This is the first time and last time (as of this writing) that Judges 19:15 has been corrupted by a Bible translation in this way.

Romans 10:9 (NIV)

If you declare with your mouth,
"Jesus is Lord,"
and believe in your heart that God
raised him from the dead, you will be saved.

If you want to accept Jesus
into your heart right now,
read the following **out loud**.

Lord Jesus, I know

you died on the cross

and that God

raised you from the dead.